ENDORSEMENTS

A mom's love. A daughter's example. A story of unconditional love. From the start, Darla Stone's book *Inside the Shadow* captivated my heart and soul. Her gripping story of God's love, grace, and mercy ignited this prayer... "God, help me see You inside the shadows of my life and view my circumstances through Your eyes not mine." Thank you, Darla, for following God's call to write your story for His glory.

—Carla McDougal, International Speaker and Blogger
Founder of Reflective Life Ministries, Author of My Prayer
Chair and Sold Out

Scripture says, "Even though I walk through the darkest valley, I will not be afraid. You are with me" (Psalm 23:4). Darla Stone shows us this truth in her honest book *Inside the Shadow*. Her story will both make your heart ache, and give you fresh outlooks by combining it with her own faith journey. Since I am a hospice chaplain, I consider this book a helpful bereavement resource. Since I lost my wife in a car accident, I am grateful for Darla's careful yet honest approach to pain, suffering, and grief.

—Jason Mirikitani, Mile Marker 825,
www.ourRescuer.com

It is difficult to paint a beautiful picture of tragedy, but that is what Darla Stone has done. She retells a truly inspirational story of what it is like to walk with a loved one through the final season of their life. With great wisdom and clarity she shows through Scripture God's deep love and father's heart toward us. Pastors, counselors, and chaplains will find this to be a helpful resource as they minister to those looking to sustain their faith through dark seasons. As a hospice chaplain, I highly recommend this book to caregivers and anyone else who is looking for inspiration and guidance from someone who has walked courageously down the path of grief.

—*Jason Sandefer*

INSIDE THE

SHADOW

INSIDE THE SHADOW

A Grief Journey

DARLA STONE

LUCIDBOOKS

Inside the Shadow

© Darla Stone

Published by Lucid Books in Houston, TX.
www.LucidBooks.net

ISBN 10: 1632960508
ISBN 13: 978-1-63296-050-4
eISBN 10: 1632960516
eISBN 13: 978-1-63296-051-1

Special Sales: Most Lucid Books titles are available in special quantity discounts. Custom imprinting or excerpting can also be done to fit special needs. Contact Lucid Books at info@lucidbooks.net.

All references to scripture are from the NASB, unless otherwise noted.

DEDICATION

This book is dedicated to redeeming the suffering by encouraging others.

"Blessed be the God and Father of our Lord Jesus Christ,
the Father of mercies and God of all comfort who
comforts us in all our affliction, so that we will
be able to comfort those who are in any affliction with the
comfort with which we ourselves are comforted by God."

– 2 Corinthians 1:3-4

ACKNOWLEDGMENTS

With much gratitude, I thank my Lord Jesus, who is "near to the brokenhearted and saves those who are crushed in spirit" (Psalm 34:18).

I also appreciate the valuable wisdom and counsel of Hank Tate and Rich Chislea. I joyfully thank my Launch Team for the many hours of reading and insightful feedback: Lynn McLeod, Jennifer Jones, Melinda Daricek, Susie Wozniak, Jacque Chislea, Tracy Stiff, and Marisa Evermon. I am grateful to Marge McCoy for always believing in this project and encouraging me to finish it.

CONTENTS

INTRODUCTION

The glass shattered into tiny pieces across the kitchen floor. As my three-year-old daughter, Erica, was getting down from her breakfast stool, the glass had inadvertently come with her. I quickly lifted her to safety outside the kitchen doorway where Kristen, 18 months old, had come running, full of curiosity. Instructions were given to keep out and cleanup ensued while little eyes watched.

Two days later, as I leaned into the back of the refrigerator, I jerked in pain as my toe connected with a large piece of broken glass beneath the grill plate. Apparently, my cleanup was not complete! Within a nano second the thought came to me, *I'm so glad this glass didn't find its way into the toes of my babies. I'm so glad it was me and not them. They are safe and all is well.*

Most mother's hearts are like that, aren't they? We love our little ones, we protect them, and we would prefer to take the pain in their place. My babies were precious to me. I had held them in my heart years before I met and married John. As a teen, I had dreamed of being a mother and had written out the names of my children yet to be. I was so grateful to be the mother of these two precious little girls. And later, I was grateful to adopt two special needs children, Carl and Rebecca, to take into my heart and raise. I was thankful for each as they came, immediately launching a study of their blueprints with the goal of knowing them inside and out.

Our family passed through the toddler years and onto childhood with the typical minor bumps, scrapes, and chicken pox. We rediscovered the beauty of God's world through a child's eyes, from fistfuls of squished wildflowers to dried worms in a pocket. During a rainstorm, Kristen announced, "When I get to heaven, I'm going to ask God if I can do the rain!" Sweet memories, even the tough ones, like hearing Carl scream with regret from the bathroom, "My got fire! My got fire!" when he had lit a match on his fingernail.

Erica was in junior high when we moved during a heavy snowstorm to our new home in Chicago. Our children delighted in the falling snow, rolling around in it like bear cubs. In Chicago, we loved the Lincoln Park Zoo, the lake front on the Fourth of July, and winter youth retreats in the snow. We drove carloads of young people to Moody Bible Institute for youth events called Second Saturday. We also drove miles to both cross-country and track meets. One very late evening, when picking Kristen up from an out-of-town track meet, I told her it was always a pleasure for me to venture out—day or night—for my children. I would never regret the journey. The summer before Erica's senior year, we moved back to Houston. John's career is in the energy industry and the move was a great opportunity for him.

Through the school years there were only a few broken bones and stitches. I rejoiced over their journey to adulthood. They had come out unscathed! As a mother bird guards her eggs in the nest, I had guarded my own young and observed as they grew stronger and began stretching their wings. And, when the time came, my birds began to leave the nest and take flight.

The month that Erica graduated from high school, she left Houston to work at a summer camp in Wisconsin, after which she planned to attend college in Chicago. Because of my belief in God, I often wrote my thoughts and prayers to God in a journal. That day, I wrote,

> Thank you, Jesus, for my family that You gave to me. I do love them so much. It is hard to ache and long for a child to love and to raise. Then the joy is felt as you receive this gift; and now I know it is a short time of life. Now the gift that I longed for—and was given—is gone. I must realize my children are temporary gifts—love and invest in them but remember they will go. They will only be with me for a short while. I face this day with Erica gone and this major part of my life over. She is my beautiful rosebud that You gave me to treasure and to raise. I know it is time for her to begin her life. Please help me to remember that and ease my heartache of not having her with me anymore.

A few years later, Erica met Jonathan at Bible school and, soon after, they happily married. Carl moved into a group home and we became his advocate rather than his main support system. Kristen made her way through Sam Houston State University and we were sure her "happily ever after" was about to begin.

John and I had just one special bird left in the nest, Rebecca. As soon as Rebecca learned to stand, she began running and climbing. I would often find her on the top pantry shelf. One day, I found her on the opposite side of the balcony that overlooked our living room. I quietly talked her into climbing back to safety as I triple-jumped the stairs to get to her. She is full of laughter and giddiness. Now, as an adult, Rebecca excels in Special Olympics Volleyball and Equestrian events.

Our "hands-on" parenting, with all its weaknesses and strengths, was coming to a close. As a mother, I felt satisfied that we had accomplished the task set before us. Through it all, I remained grateful—so grateful—that God had given me these precious ones. They were healthy and vibrant and they knew Jesus. They were ready to live their own lives and I was willing to let go!

Could I release each one? I was to find that releasing Kristen to adulthood and marriage and to God would be more difficult than I could fathom.

Chapter One

BLISS AND BEWILDERMENT

The sun comes up, it's a new day dawning
It's time to sing Your song again.
Whatever may pass and whatever lies before me,
let me be singing when the evening comes.

Bless the Lord, oh my soul
oh my soul, worship His holy name
sing like never before, oh my soul
I worship Your holy name.[1]

The day after Kristen died I went into my closet and fell to my knees in crushing, staggering sorrow. Wails of profound anguish rose from deep within me. I truly believed I would not get up from the closet floor. The heartbeat that had been formed within me had stopped, and the gaping wound it had left would surely cause my own heartbeat to cease. Can a mother continue to live when her child dies? I thought not. I believed this sorrow would bring my death. In fact, I preferred to think of death for myself, rather than the unbearable grief that was encompassing me. Yet, my lungs continued to take in air and my heart continued to beat.

It seemed a lifetime ago; yet, just four years earlier, celebration was in the air! Kristen was graduating from Sam Houston State University on a crisp, cool day in December, which is rare and refreshing for the humid Gulf Coast of Texas. Photos from that day reveal my husband, John, and I both beaming with joy. There was no hint of what lay ahead—just photos of happiness with our oldest daughter, Erica, and her husband, Jonathan, along with our youngest daughter, Rebecca, all celebrating Kristen's big day. David, Kristen's boyfriend, was by her side to celebrate the day.

Kristen and David had met during their senior year of high school and dated briefly during the summer before they left for college. During Kristen's first weekend visit home that September, David ended their close friendship. Through her tears, Kristen told John, "It's so strange because I thought David was the one for me."

They continued their separate ways throughout college. One January day, about five years later, our entire family was leaving church together. John's sister, Sherry, and her family were with us. In the parking lot, we heard someone call Kristen's name. Kristen turned and walked toward him, while Sherry and I curiously peeked around the car. I told her, "That's David, who broke Kristen's heart." My thoughts had not dwelt on David during the past five years, but I had given him a label—the one who broke Kristen's heart. A few weeks later, Kristen told me they were still talking and that David had apologized. David then, very sincerely, spoke alone to John and me. He said a few things, but the line I recall most dearly is, "I will not break Kristen's heart again." Within a few months, they began dating exclusively.

The night of Kristen's graduation, when family and friends joined for a celebratory dinner, David stepped out to speak to John about his intentions. Later that night Kristen was engaged to be married! Within the next two months, Kristen would turn 24 and become a newlywed.

We were all quickly immersed in blissful planning. A flurry followed. China pattern chosen. Showers of celebrations and gifts bestowed. A beautiful white dress with satin ballerina shoes! A candlelit, country chapel on a starry night! Friends and family beaming as the newlyweds danced.

John and I both believe that marriage releases the ties of hands-on parenting. We had released Erica to Jonathan's responsibility five years earlier. As a mother, I looked forward to the same progression for Kristen as Erica had experienced—a transition away from us and into her new life of marriage and family. Kristen and David were a couple and we trusted David to take the lead.

Life was one joyous event after another. That spring, Erica gave birth to her second child, Megan. After substituting for one semester, Kristen began the school year with her own first grade class. She looked forward to pouring herself into her students. I happily joined her in decorating her classroom, attaching apple name tags to a paper tree on the bulletin board and creating a cozy book corner.

That September, I prepared for a ten-day mission trip to Russia, where I would be teaching women at a leaders' conference a Bible Study I had written. I was grateful—always grateful—that God had called me to be His and that He used me for His Kingdom. In November, I thoroughly enjoyed the experience. Siberia was a winter wonderland. I was invited to return to Russia the next year and present a second study. I gladly accepted and looked forward to the planning and the research.

However, our lives took a different direction upon my return. Kristen told John and me that she had discovered a lump on her breast. She had already met with our family doctor and scheduled a mammogram. A few days later, Kristen was told to follow up in six months with a second mammogram. The lump did not concern her. Kristen rarely operated in urgency mode. Her words to me were, "Mother, I'm 24—I'll be just fine!" I was uneasy about waiting and comforted myself in thinking that all problems would be solved in six months.

When the sixth month follow-up time came in May, I asked Kristen if she had made the appointment. She had not scheduled the appointment because the hectic schedule of the school year ending had taken priority. The lump would have to wait. When we were talking that day, Kristen shared with me that the lump had doubled, seeming to form a barbell-type shape. Frantically, I said, "Let me feel that! Kristen, you don't mess around with lumps! Make an appointment!" Yet, she still did not feel compelled to make an appointment. The lump was a minute detail in an active life. Kristen's life was full because she was where she had dreamed of since childhood—that happily ever after place!

Kristen and David were typical young newlyweds with the belief that together they were invincible. They were bulletproof! The newlyweds jumped adventurously into everything. Just one aspect of their energetic lives was to fill Sunday afternoons as leadership volunteers with the Junior High students at their church. Kristen looked forward to the summer when her schedule would lighten and she could do even more with the young people. The first of June, immediately after school ended, Kristen was packing to join and chaperone the youth for a week-long wilderness adventure trip.

Trips like this were characteristic of Kristen. Throughout high school and college, she had participated in eight mission trips, both as a student and later as a youth counselor. One trip was a six-week summer odyssey with Campus Crusade in the Middle East. She related the following thoughts in her journal:

> Such a day of mixed emotions and, yet, it ended so wonderfully. Here I am in Jordan lounging on a thin mattress, listening to praise music. The windows are open and we are waiting for the breeze to cool us off—as this is called the 'cool breeze' room. This morning I woke up feeling drained and wasted. I couldn't make myself go out on campus. Then I was chosen to lead our Celebration of Discipline discussion for tonight and I was overwhelmed with feelings of inadequacy. But the Lord has taken care of me and brought me to Himself in

worship. The discussion time ended up being wonderful and I had a great time praising the Lord in song tonight. The Lord did not leave me in the pit of despair but He lifted me up to Himself.

I thank God that Kristen held a strong belief in the truth of God. I was grateful that she did invest time in knowing Him and sharing His truth to others. It came as no surprise to me that she would follow through on her commitment to the junior high wilderness trip that June.

So, rather than scheduling a recheck of her lump, Kristen left on a bus for the wilderness. Feeling an overwhelming inner mom-sense of urgency, I asked if she would allow me to make the follow-up appointment for her. The wilderness trip ended on a Sunday; so I made the appointment for Monday morning. A mammogram was done the following week and the proverbial snowball began a rapid roll down the mountain.

After that, a specialist was called and a biopsy was taken in early July. The movie scene of sitting in a doctor's office hearing biopsy results did not play out for Kristen. The doctor insensitively called her when she was home alone with the news that she had breast cancer. She called David at work and he began racing home. She then called me crying. For 10 minutes, I stood in my kitchen, talking and praying with her until David was by her side. Incredibly, I had to teach the final session of a series to women that evening. Disbelief and shock buffered my senses, and I was able to speak.

I had taken pride in releasing my children, but suddenly thoughts of release were in extreme reverse. The inner mom-sense of urgency was overpowering and gaining strength within me. Like a mother bear, wanting to protect her cub, I ferociously wanted to bring Kristen back into my den and shield her from harm.

I longed to return to the years when my child was in my home, a place where I seemed to remember having more control. A place where I could kiss wounds, pull out a Band-Aid and wipe the tears away. A place where I could sweep away the broken juice glass and make my child safe once again. A place where I could make a quick appointment with a doctor and get a ten-day prescription for my young charge.

It seemed as though an infinitesimal shard of broken glass was piercing into my heart. I felt shock–perhaps the diagnosis was incorrect. I felt uneasy–yet reassured myself that there were advances and cures in cancer treatment. As any mother does for her child, I felt an overwhelming distress for my child's own feelings. I cried for her. I prayed for her. I didn't want her dreams to be broken or waylaid.

A missionary from our church was going through cancer treatment at about the same time and posted the following on his website:

> With cancer, one loses control over the health of their body, over planning the future, even the simple plans of the day ahead. The truth is that people believe they are in control when they actually are not. The beauty, if you would call it that, of this cancer, is that you are forced to realize that you are not in control and you have been given the opportunity to live like

that. People who accept the state of not being in control do much better in handling the illness. Let us learn to live each day with peace in our hearts by trusting the only One Who is in control.

Throughout all of the uneasiness of this dark tunnel we were entering, I maintained one positive feeling—**I felt secure in God**. I didn't consciously speak these words to everyone I knew—I just felt safe. I knew God walked with me in whatever journey my life would take. I began to remind myself—with daily concerted effort—to release the ferocious mother bear in me and purposely shift focus to my Shepherd. As a young lamb in the pasture hears the shepherd's voice and heeds, years ago I had learned to know Jesus Christ. I didn't desire—in any way—to traverse this unknown path; it seemed I was a lamb being asked to walk on the edge of a treacherous cliff filled with boulders! Yet, my Shepherd was with me; He called and I followed, bleating as I went!

Chapter Two

IS IT REALLY CANCER?

I was sure by now
God, You would have reached down
and wiped our tears away
stepped in and saved the day.
But, once again, I say 'amen,' and it's still raining.

And I'll praise You in this storm
and I will lift my hands
for You are who You are
no matter where I am.[2]

I awoke the day after Kristen's diagnosis and thought perhaps a second test would clear up the misunderstanding. I hoped that God would avert this impending journey. Yet, we moved forward. The sense of urgency that I had had for the past few months was suddenly felt by this young couple. The diagnosis was given, and we needed to find an oncologist. David made an appointment at MD Anderson Cancer

Research Center, a leader in the nation for cancer research and, fortunately, ten minutes from where Kristen lived. However, the wait for an appointment was set for three weeks.

We desperately wanted clarification sooner! We wanted a second opinion, now! David was able to procure an appointment at a different facility on the far west side of Houston the next day. The doctor we met with was very knowledgeable and able to help us comprehend the enormity that Kristen faced.

Eight months after first making its appearance known, the lumpy intruder was given a name. The oncologist explained to us that this insidious cancer was named invasive ductal carcinoma with HER2 gene amplification. In 2002, this was known to be the most aggressive form of breast cancer. We were told that researchers had isolated this gene and created a "smart drug" that halted the growth of the tumors. However, FDA regulators were insisting on more research. Herceptin, the new "smart drug," was only to be given when the cancer metastasized (moved to other parts of her body). Kristen's tumors were found in her left breast and several lymph nodes. At this point, because there was no sign of cancer elsewhere in her body, she was not eligible for the drug. Due to the aggressive nature of this cancer, the doctor advised Kristen to begin with an immediate mastectomy followed by chemo treatment. We left the appointment in shock, attempting to process what had been said.

After that second opinion, David still determined that the better place to treat Kristen's cancer was MD Anderson. Friends and family had begun to pray for a sooner appointment than three weeks. Incredibly, connections with someone from their church who had been praying were made. David received a call and, within three days, Kristen, David, and I were sitting in the waiting room for her first appointment.

I immediately began writing the foreign words and phrases that the oncologist relayed to us. A protocol was set that began with one chemotherapy drug called Taxol for three months to be followed by three months of a second chemo called FEC. The next part of the plan would be a mastectomy. After recovering from that surgery, ten weeks of radiation treatment would follow. I began to calculate. The snowball had begun rolling rapidly in June after Kristen's wilderness trip. It was now August. I calculated that Kristen's schedule was to be realigned for the next ten months. Kristen's life had been hijacked but by next June she would surely be free—the cancer would be gone.

Because both David and Kristen dreamed of a large family, they sought advice from a fertility doctor. David comes from a very large family of sixteen and looked forward to being a dad. As a child, Kristen had drawn pictures of her future babies, and as a young teen she had cut out pictures from magazines to design her future home when she would marry and make all those babies! When Kristen had her first summer job, she walked into the house one day with a shopping bag. She pulled out a beautiful blue outfit for a baby boy and announced that the gift was for her future son. Kristen joined in our reaction of laughter toward her future plans. She then tucked the outfit away for her child yet to be.

The desire for children ran deep in both Kristen and David. The fertility specialist told them that precautions should be taken to freeze several eggs because there was a chance that chemo could induce menopause. When they learned that taking such measures would delay the start of treatment by two months, they chose to put the matter of their children in God's hands and begin treatment immediately.

Soon after Kristen was diagnosed, I had a frightening dream. My husband, Kristen, and I were walking through what seemed to be an airport. As we walked together, I noted an escalator. I passed by, yet I sensed Kristen was not with me. I looked back and she was ascending the escalator. In my dream I felt uneasy, yet I knew she would come back down, once she realized her mistake. I ran to find a descending escalator and could not find one. Panic set in as I ran, and I began calling to John to search for her. I could sense time passing quickly. I woke from this dream crying and facing the reality that Kristen's future was unknown. I cried out to God for His mercy and asked Him to allow her to live. The next day, as I relayed the dream to John, I told him that I could physically feel my heart breaking.

We now had clarification. With each appointment, the diagnosis of breast cancer wrapped itself around us like an unwanted vine slowly threatening to choke us. Shock was replaced by reality. We were on a journey into the unknown world of cancer treatment. The infinitesimal shard of broken glass in my heart was beginning to cause large jagged edges.

I wondered at God's wisdom in this choice of cancer for my daughter. As many of us do, I thought I could actually run a better scenario than God had chosen. The mother should get the cancer, not the child! I thought, "I'm 50; I have lived my 'ever after' dreams; it would be more logical to give me the cancer. My child's dreams have just begun; she is too young!

She is just beginning her great adventure!" The true scenario in which we found ourselves was unfathomable to me. I could only see the cancer and the accompanying physical suffering as a colossal interruption of a well-lived life. I fervently prayed for the same outcome that the apostle Paul had once written about his friend: "For indeed he was sick to the point of death, but God had mercy on him, and not on him only but also on me, lest I should have sorrow upon sorrow" (Philippians 2:27).

Friends of ours had business cards printed with Kristen's picture and a short description of her cancer. "We have fixed our hope on the living God" was printed at the bottom. We gave these cards to everyone we knew, asking for prayer. I do fix my hope on the living God. As I stated earlier, I had come to know the truth of God as a young child, and I trusted in that truth. The truth is that God loves each person on earth with an everlasting, overwhelming love.

The Bible teaches that "all have sinned and fall short of the glory of God" (Romans 3:23). God abhors sin and has given a sentence of eternal death to those who sin. Yet, God did not leave mankind helpless and hopeless in this fallen state of sin. He chose to take the sentence of death away through His Son. Jesus took the place of mankind and was willing to die eternally so all could live. John 3:16 explains, "For God so loved the world that He gave His only begotten Son, that whoever believes in Him will not perish, but have everlasting life." The phrase "will not perish" refers to eternal perishing. Those who place their belief in Jesus Christ will live eternally with Him though they physically die.

There are some who, upon hearing that all have sinned, see only that they are being condemned by God. John 3:17

further explains, "For God did not send the Son into the world to judge the world, but that the world might be saved through Him." Not one person comes into life loving and knowing God. God loves us regardless of our response to Him. Yet, He desires that all who hear the truth will respond in belief.

Belief in the sacrifice of Christ ushers in a hope from God that does not disappoint because He lavishly pours His love into us. This is not a hope that tomorrow will be a sunny day. It is not a hope that my favorite team will win the championship.

My hope in the living God is that He promises to hear me when I pray. My hope is that He does answer prayer. He calls me His child and He will comfort me when I hurt. He will give me strength when I am weak. He will never leave me nor forsake me. He holds me in the palm of His hand. He promises me a future with Him beyond my imagination. My hope is in the living God. I can gladly share that my family places their hope in the living God, as well. The business cards expressed our hearts.

Chapter Three

MD ANDERSON

Day by day, and with each passing moment
strength I find to meet my trials here;
trusting in my Father's wise bestowment
I've no cause for worry or for fear.
He whose heart is kind beyond all measure
gives unto each day what He deems best.
Lovingly, its part of pain and pleasure
mingling toil with peace and rest.[3]

MD Anderson Cancer Research Hospital's motto is "Making Cancer History." The collective buildings of this massive complex have a staff population that is more than my small hometown in Pennsylvania! MD Anderson is like a city within the city of Houston. It has its own post office. Within the two buildings we frequented most, there are ten cafes, a large cafeteria, and a few coffee bars. There are five gift shops with varied specialty items. A hair salon is open to patients who still have hair and provides an array of wigs, hats, and scarves for those who don't. A grand piano is located in the lobby which comes to life throughout any given day by many gifted volunteers. Massive fish tanks are set strategically throughout the buildings to give an ambiance of tranquility. Volunteers set up random massage stations to soothe stressed neck and shoulder muscles.

I found the people in this small city to be very kind. The accommodations were welcoming and comfortable. However, I noted everything in passing. I was simply grateful to be with my daughter. One of the oncologists had taken pictures of Kristen, David, and myself for her files. I was an official support team member. I sat by my daughter's side taking notes at appointments. Wild horses could not have dragged me away from day-long diagnostic tests and treatments!

The day of her first chemo treatment, Kristen had a titanium port placed into her upper chest at a separate day-surgery facility. Attached to the port is a catheter which leads directly into a vein so that the chemo can spread efficiently and quickly through a patient's body. Although this is known as minor surgery, it did not feel minor. We felt nervous and unsure as we moved forward. We were learning terms we could barely grasp. The port also did not appear minor to us. It looked like a raised quarter beneath her skin. It was late afternoon when the anesthesia wore off. We left the day surgery and immediately went to the chemo appointment at MD Anderson.

The nurse connected the chemo to the new port, checked the gauges, and left Kristen, David, and me alone. Within a few minutes, Kristen said she felt strange. A red flush appeared on her face and quickly began to spread over her body, sending David frantically running for the nurse. Within a few moments, he returned with the nurse to find Kristen the color of a pickled beet from head to toe. The nurse immediately stopped the chemo intake and explained that Kristen was experiencing an allergic reaction. The reaction slowly subsided as the nurse administered powerful steroids and antihistamines, and the chemo intake resumed. After several hours, we finally left the hospital. My typical 40-minute drive home was shortened, as very few cars were on the freeways at 2 a.m. I was still wide awake as I continued to absorb and process the day's hectic events.

At her home, Kristen sensed her breathing had become shallow. During the weekend, it became more difficult to breathe deeply, but she had never experienced chemo before and assumed this was another new adjustment. That Monday, a nurse called to inquire about Kristen's health after the first chemo treatment. Kristen mentioned her breathing difficulties and the nurse commented that shallow breathing would not be a side effect. The nurse advised Kristen to immediately return to the hospital to determine the cause of her discomfort.

After tests in the emergency room, Kristen was admitted to the hospital for several days. It was determined that her lung had accidentally been clipped during the minor port surgery and had collapsed. A chest tube was inserted between her rib cage and lungs to allow trapped air and gas to escape and enable her lung to re-inflate. Because of the chemo, steroids, and collapsed lung, Kristen had no appetite. Knowing this common side effect, MD Anderson provides an on-call menu to accommodate patients rather than the typical hospital 3-meals-a-day fare. At some point, Kristen chose tapioca pudding, a comfort food from when she was a child. The waiter arrived, dressed as though he had come from a 5-star restaurant, with the pudding on a silver covered platter!

The shock of diagnosis had begun to wear off, and the stark reality of cancer began to come full force to Kristen while she was in the hospital. I stayed by her side during the day while David was at work. She felt an anxiety that she had never experienced and realized she was entering into an unknown time of suffering.

I recalled that, several years earlier, Kristen had conversed with me at length about the subject of suffering. She had always had difficulty parting with projects and notebooks. While she was still a teen at home, we would laugh at what she had saved as we would occasionally purge her room of school papers and reports. Much later, I was grateful to find a paper on the subject of suffering that she had written while in college. I realized that she had continued to process her thoughts on suffering after our conversation. She wrote,

> Does my life have many hard trials and tribulations to come? I have often asked myself this question. For a time, I was afraid to live my life because 2 Timothy 3:12 guarantees Christians a life of persecution. This means trials and tribulations. I don't want to hurt. I don't want to cry. I don't want the pain.

> As I read through the Bible, I discover that trials and tribulations produce characteristics and qualities that we need. The trials will bring about perseverance, proven character, and

hope. Our Lord wants us to be continually dependent on Him. I do not know what trials and tribulations my life will hold. Only God knows. I don't want to fear living. God is in control and working to conform me to His image. If being totally dependent on my Father means suffering, then I must suffer, because I want nothing more than to be completely dependent on my Father.

Nearly six years after she had contemplated an unknown suffering, Kristen was living out the process. Although she had written that she did not want to hurt or cry or experience pain, she was hurting and crying and in pain. Would this trial produce new character traits in her as she had also written? Would she become more dependent on God? Time would tell.

Life took on a new normal. Blood level checks were routine, and, if the levels were within an adequate range, chemo followed. If her white blood count was not high enough, chemo would be postponed for a week. The following week, the tests would be repeated. The delays did occur a few times throughout her chemo treatment. I tried not to think of the cancer cells gathering strength to rebuild and launch attacks on her body when this happened.

Of course, nausea and loss of appetite then followed the chemo. After the second chemo treatment, Kristen's long, beautiful hair fell out in clumps. A friend shaved the bits that were left on her scalp. A piece of my child's original blueprint was gone, with the final sweep of the razor. Kristen quit her teaching job to be cautious with her weakened immune system.

Sweet, happy first graders who love to hug are so loaded with germs! To keep expenses down, they also sold the car that she had recently purchased. One aspect that they didn't give up was the junior high youth ministry. It was encouraging to know that the students and their families rallied around this young couple.

Throughout all of this, I would report details to John. He didn't come with us to the appointments because, of course, he was working. But he did feel an overwhelming hopelessness as a father. Like the proverbial knight in shining armor, he had always been able to come to the rescue. When she broke her finger as a child at the playground, Kristen had been scooped into her daddy's arms and driven to the hospital.

John had come alongside Kristen in her joys, as well. When Kristen took up running as a teen, John joined in. They ran together through our neighborhood. He volunteered one year when Kristen participated in a Junior Olympics running team. Her team made the national level that year, and they drove to Florida together for the competition. Years later, when she called him panicked over a blown tire, John calmed her as he drove an hour through city traffic to her rescue. Now a powerful, unknown disease had overtaken his charge, his child. Adding to the helplessness was the fact that Kristen was no longer a child and no longer his charge. John had become a knight immobilized.

During that time, I wrote in my journal,

> I have a memory of being very young and riding in the car at night with my parents. I recall the evening shadows made by trees in

the moonlight. I remember feeling content and safe as my father drove. Now, at this great place of the unknown future, I truly want to trust God most, more than any human on earth. I want to feel the same as I did in the car as a child—content and safe—as my Father God controls Kristen's life. Father, if this sickness is needed to fulfill Your purpose and glory in my life or in someone else, please don't take it away. I pray Mary's words, "I am the Lord's servant and I am willing to accept whatever He wants."

The words of Mary occurred when she was told that she would become the mother of Jesus. She did not totally comprehend what was being asked of her, but she accepted God's plan. I desired to do the same. I viewed Kristen's "sickness" as a temporary assignment of both suffering and growth—something in which we, as a family, could tangibly see victory. We would move on and look back years later at how we had grown.

However, as time continued and the suffering worsened, I struggled with what I had written in the journal. Reality of the physical and emotional suffering was overpowering. I felt shocked that I could have so easily considered praying that God would not take the sickness away. Questions began to surface: What was I thinking? How long would we be in this? How much suffering? Where exactly was God taking my child? Taking me? I wished for details before I moved forward, yet I knew I had to live out each day not knowing the answers to my questions.

A phrase from a popular praise song at the time by Toby Mac would ring in my ears, "Anything, I would give up for You; everything, I'd give it all away."[4] Every time I heard the song, the words would haunt my thoughts. Could I really "give it all away?" Could I give up my agenda of victory over cancer? Could I continue accepting whatever God had for us, as Mary did? I felt overcome with weakness. I needed God's supernatural strength because mine was fading fast! God promises His supernatural strength will give us strength when we are weak. I could not bear to look too far into the future. I was very sure I could only do one thing—get through one day at a time!

Chapter Four

FRIENDLY ADVICE

At this my heart trembles, and leaps from its place.
Listen closely to the Lord's voice, and the rumbling
that goes out from His mouth...whether for correction,
or for His world, or for loving kindness,
He causes it to happen.

Job 37:1-2, 13

Soon after Kristen's cancer diagnosis, friends and families began to call. Many called to say they were sorry and they were praying. We gained strength in knowing others prayed for us. Kristen and I met with a few women who had survived breast cancer. They shared their stories and helped prepare the way for the treacherous journey Kristen faced. We were touched and grateful that so many cared for and supported us.

Some friends called suggesting alternative treatment plans. A few friends sent cases of vitamins and herbal drinks.

Others urged David and Kristen to fly to alternative treatment centers in Mexico and Colorado. One caller gave the address, date, and time that Kristen could go to a faith healer.

I opened an email one morning from an acquaintance who had searched backward for the cause of Kristen's cancer and drew a conclusion. She was quick to offer advice. Old Testament verses filled this email and suggested that Kristen should confess her sins and be healed. It is true that, at times, God allows suffering as a natural consequence of one's own choices. I do agree there is truth in the statement that a person may experience spiritual and emotional healing through confessing their sin. However, if this becomes the formulaic answer for all suffering, we might just be placing God in a box. God has told us that His ways are not our ways. God has told us that He is incomprehensible and unfathomable.

There are times that we encounter suffering and cannot fathom the "why" of it. We are not alone in this quest. For thousands of years, many have asked "why" did disaster strike or a loved one become sick. In the Bible, Gideon once asked, "If the Lord is with us, why has all this happened to us?" (Judges 6:13). Also found in the Bible is the account of Job, found in the book by the same name. His suffering was tremendous, so his three friends went to console him. Together, they spent most of their visit searching for the cause of Job's suffering. At length, they dissected Job's life, searching for a deficit in Job's faith. Their conclusions sounded much like the email I received.

At times, God allows events to occur in our lives in order to reveal to us a facet of His character that we might not grasp by any other means than through the particular crisis we are in. Jesus teaches us this important truth in John 9:1-3. The disciples of Jesus pointed to a man born blind and asked Him, "Who sinned, this man or his parents? Jesus answered, 'Neither this man nor his parents sinned, but this happened so that the work of God might be displayed in him.'" Suffering may just be so that all involved can witness the glory of God. In any event, suffering accomplishes a greater purpose.

When any suffering does come, should we take the time and emotional energy to examine why? Author Philip Yancey states, "The disciples wanted to look backward, to find out 'why'. To backward looking questions of cause there often is no definitive answer. A human tragedy can be used simply to display God's work."[5] Whatever the cause, our response can bring glory to God.

The phone calls continued, sometimes with odd questions, such as asking if David would "stick by" Kristen since they were just newlyweds. Most of the calls included one common question: Are you or Kristen angry with God? I began to wonder why so many wanted to know. Was it just a need to know a person's response to cancer? Did curiosity or concern or fear cause this question to surface? Was there a perception that cancer diagnosis qualifies one to be angry?

It is true that we can feel helpless, hopeless, sadness, fear, and anger all at once when facing the harsh reality of suffering. Any of these emotions are healthy and normal to feel. Many don't want to accept that physical suffering is the harsh reality of this world, until it becomes personal. When suffering became personal for Job, he asked, "Shall we indeed accept good from God and not accept adversity?" (Job 2:10).

These are truths that I learned from the Bible. They became beliefs that I held and had been teaching others for many years. I was now being field tested. In this incredible test of my child's cancer, would I continue to believe that the Bible held the truth? I believe the unspoken question from the calls and comments was really, "Can the faith anchor hold in the sea of adversity?"

I definitely felt the harsh reality of adversity was slamming into me like a freight train! Suffering had become personal for me. I wasn't spouting deep spiritual answers at this point, but I was surely hearing from a lot of people who wanted to know. My mind was overflowing in continuous crisis mode. I felt many emotions. I felt overwhelmed because our lives had taken an abrupt turn. I felt an urgency in grasping the rapid intake of medical terminology—rushing to my computer after every doctor's appointment, hoping to comprehend through Google what was said. I felt lost driving through the city searching and backtracking for hospital parking garages and then through hallway mazes. I felt uncertain that the absolute best decisions were being made to eradicate cancer from my daughter's body. I felt heartsick as I watched chemo drip into my child. I felt afraid of this journey—the unknown length of it and where it might lead.

There was one emotion that I did not feel. I did not feel angry at God. I was clinging to God! I had eagerly accepted that He loved me as a very young child, just as He loves all the children of the world. I learned this through my Sunday morning teachers. When I was eleven, I had tearfully accepted His forgiveness through Jesus Christ, and I knew He would be a part of my life forever. During the confusing early days of Kristen's diagnosis, when I had a quiet moment to focus on God, I would simply ask of Him two things: please heal

Kristen and please hold me while I wait. Through Jesus, God is our "Abba Father," a term which means "daddy." I just wanted to sit on my Abba Daddy's lap and be held. What better place to turn for comfort when crying? Believe me, I cried—a lot! I longed for tunnel vision focused on Him alone to give me strength.

Kristen shared that she had been receiving similar calls asking whether she were angry with God. She had experienced a swift, unceremonious change of a planned life. Kristen was uncertain and afraid. But she was not angry. She shared with me that she was crying out to God. Kristen was running to Jesus for comfort. She was leaning into God for comfort and strength. She showed me a verse card that she carried with her.

> Hear my cry, O God; give heed to my prayer. From the end of the earth I call to Thee, when my heart is faint. Lead me to the rock that is higher than I. For Thou hast been a refuge for me, a tower of strength against the enemy.
> *(Psalm 61: 1-3)*

Between the calls, the questions, and the influx of medical decisions, Kristen relied more heavily on David. She came to a point in time when she did not want to answer the questions or listen to the unsolicited advice. David rose to the task of protecting and providing for his wife courageously. He began responding to the well-meaning calls that Kristen had been receiving. He focused on decision making.

He was Kristen's closest confidant, and he became her most avid cheerleader. He brought laughter to our hospital visits. The three of us would be waiting in a small room for a doctor. David would open a drawer and find a detailed brochure of the breast and cancer. He would place the brochure in the lighted x-ray display on the wall. With pen as a pointer, David would explain the breast to us in quasi-medical terms. His antics lightened the heaviness of our visits. Doctors typically entered the room to find us suppressing laughter.

In my longing for that tunnel vision, an old hymn played through my mind:

Be Thou my vision, O Lord of my heart
naught be all else to me, save that Thou are.
Thou my best thought, by day or by night.
Waking or sleeping, Thy Presence my light.

High King of Heaven, my victory won.
May I reach Heaven's joy, O bright Heaven's Sun!
Heart of my own heart, whatever befall,
still be my vision, O Ruler of all.[6]

Chapter Five

ONE STEP FORWARD, TWO STEPS BACK

All who sail the sea of faith
find out before too long
how quickly blue skies can grow dark
and gentle winds grow strong
Suddenly, fear is like white water
pounding on the soul.
Still, we sail on knowing
that our Lord is in control.
Sometimes, He calms the storm
with a whispered, "Peace, be still."

He can settle any sea
but it doesn't mean He will.
Sometimes, He holds us close
and lets the wind and waves go wild.
Sometimes, He calms the storm
and, other times, He calms His child.[7]

Christmas was coming! The tree was decorated, presents were wrapped, and cookies were baked! Kristen had finished her first three months of chemotherapy with Taxol and one month of the second type called FEC. A feeling of optimism prevailed because the scans indicated that the tumors were visibly shrinking. We believed we were moving forward in the battle to destroy the cancer cells!

The entire family gathered to celebrate the birth of Jesus. Kristen and David drove up from their home in Houston. Erica and her family drove in from their home in San Antonio. Carl joined us from his group home. In our family, the celebration always extends through December 28, Kristen's birthday. On her 26th birthday, I was grateful and reminiscing about this second child of mine. She was due before Christmas but chose to make her appearance after her due date. My sweet child was born with silky, straight, golden hair. Her hair was so straight that her ears would easily poke through the strands. Kristen was born in Olean, New York, and came home to her older sister, Erica. Soon after, our family began an odyssey of five major moves across the country to further John's career. Three of the moves were into, and out of, Houston, Texas, where we currently live.

During our first stay in Houston, we adopted Carl, and, years later in Chicago, Rebecca. One benefit of all the moves was the close relationship that developed between Erica and Kristen. Searching to find a friend in each new location was not easily done, but Kristen never had to say goodbye to her best friend, Erica.

Words to describe Kristen's youth are adventurous, fun-loving, risk-taking, and athletic. She loved climbing trees. As early as five years old, Kristen had conquered the 25-foot tree in our front yard. When we moved to Chicago, her fourth grade class did not readily accept the new girl who showed up in January. One day in PE class, the students were asked to climb a rope suspended from the gym ceiling, and they huddled together trying to gather courage. Because Kristen was excluded from the conversation, she simply grabbed the rope and climbed to the top of the gym before someone noticed and shrieked. Later, she overheard a boy from her class extolling her athletic ability to someone on the playground. She found her best fit in long distance running both in track and cross country. Kristen broke a state record in her freshman year of high school in Illinois during cross country.

Climbing and running continued to define Kristen. She wrote in her journal when she was eighteen and on her third mission trip to Mexico,

> We are in Guanajuato and a group of us woke up at 3 a.m, to climb Mt. Bob. We start off in the dark like this every year, and this year we had the moon to light our way. We go through some hard parts to get to the foot of the mountain. We slide down a huge, 50-ft. long gravel pit and then walk straight up the mountain. You are on your own and sometimes have to grab onto anything just to pull yourself up. Your thighs and calves burn and your legs get tired. It was my third year in a row to be the first girl to make it to the top! David, Jeff, and I were the first three

there. At the top of the mountain is a cross. Once everyone gets to the top, we meet at the cross, and watch the sunrise. Then one of the adults with us leads us in communion. Our trip down the mountain is so much easier!

Through her years of running, Kristen developed self-discipline and endurance, two character traits that would serve her well when she faced the battle for her life. Of all our children, Kristen was the most energetic, physically fit, and healthy. She more readily jumped at the chance for adventure, such as the mission trips, than any of her siblings.

The mission trips were fun for her, but they were also an opportunity to share the good news of Jesus through skits and evangelizing at the local market square. From the same trip when she was eighteen, Kristen wrote in her journal,

> It was our last night in the market and we had another good turnout. Our youth pastor, Greg, had a Mexican girl translate for him. One guy continued talking to him for a long time. Most everybody went back to the mission house. I stayed with the few that were waiting for Greg and we prayed for the guy while they continued to talk. It was neat because the man became a Christian. Greg introduced us to the guy and a few of us began crying.

Now, eight years after that climb to the top of Mt. Bob, we were celebrating that Kristen was 26. On her birthday, lifelong friends came in from Beaumont. We women spent lunch at the Cheesecake Factory, laughing and remembering when the children were young. However, as we drove home, Kristen leaned over to me and whispered in my ear, "I have a new lump." Instantaneously, I could feel a heavy weight fall on my chest. Fortunately, I kept the car on the road!

The second chemo, FEC, had failed in its purpose and our optimism dissolved. We had moved one step forward, but now it seemed we were two steps back in the battle against the cancer cells. A frantic call was made to Kristen's oncologist. Within two days Kristen was being scanned again at MD Anderson. The mastectomy that had been scheduled for late January was immediately reset for New Year's Eve. During the pre-op appointment, I excused myself and found a different waiting room in which to cry. I had to hide for quite some time; it seemed I wasn't able to stop. I wanted to be strong for my child—I didn't want her to see my anguish. However, I was always finding myself to be weak.

The day of surgery, many family and friends filled the waiting room to overflowing. One friend specifically came earlier than the others to pray with us before surgery. Throughout the next few hours, I sat anxiously waiting, continuously twirling and playing with my wedding ring. Kristen was wheeled out of recovery and settled into a room. The next day I realized that I had twirled my diamond ring right off my hand somewhere at MD Anderson. We searched but never found it. I hoped it didn't get sucked into the dirt of a vacuum cleaner but, rather, that someone who needed a ring found it.

As Kristen physically recovered from the mastectomy, I emotionally grappled with the surgery results. Twenty-six years earlier, I had counted every finger and toe, thanking God for such a gift. I had spent many of those years acquainting myself with the blueprint of this child. In my thoughts, she was my baby once again, and a part of her was now missing. I ached for my little girl who sucked her thumb and loved her blankie. I cried for my child who dearly loved her dolls and her two pet rabbits. I cried for the athlete who was always physically fit.

My mind knew that Kristen was God's child and that He held her in His hand. I knew that Christ would never leave her nor forsake her. I knew there was nothing to fear. I knew if Christ called her to go to be with Him, it would be the best choice for her. Yet, at times, even with all this knowledge, sorrow and anxiety would surface and overflow. I prayed that God would restore my emotions and guard my heart as He walked me through this suffering place. I thanked God that Kristen was recovering and alive.

He has a reason for each trial
that we pass through in life
and though we're shaken,
We cannot be pulled apart from Christ,
no matter how the driving rain beats down.

On those who hold to faith,
a heart of trust will always
be a quiet, peaceful place.
Sometimes, He calms the storm
and, other times, He calms His child.[8]

Chapter Six

NO EVIDENCE OF DISEASE?

For we are powerless before this great multitude who are coming against us; nor do we know what to do, but our eyes are on Thee.

2 Chronicles 20:12

After the mastectomy on New Year's Eve, Kristen was given six weeks to recover before the final protocol of radiation began. Radiation therapy uses high-energy beams, which are invisible to the human eye, to damage a cell's DNA. In mid-February, the weekly appointments began. I had been able to sit beside her during each chemo treatment. However, radiation was a solitary time for just Kristen and the beams. I waited outside the room through each appointment, imagining the beams destroying any bits of cancer that were left in Kristen's body. The beams damage healthy cells that are in the area, as well. A large patch of skin is left parched and fragile. After several sessions, it looks and feels like a severe sunburn. After a few sessions, Kristen began to feel physically fatigued, as well.

A small dinner bell hangs in the radiation wing at MD Anderson. The tradition is to ring the bell in jubilation on the day of the final radiation treatment. Rebecca was with Kristen and me on this day. They stood together and I snapped their picture as Kristen rang the bell! Victory! Triumph! Ring that bell! No more radiation!

At the final meeting with the radiation oncologist, he stated that the radiation appeared to have eradicated tumor cells in the surrounding area of what was once Kristen's breast. The scans showed "no evidence of disease" (NED) at that time. An appointment was set for a reassessment in June to determine whether or not tumors remained gone and the NED status would remain. Tests and scans would be done at that time.

The ten months of various types of treatment were completed. However, the chemo, surgery, and radiation had left Kristen's head bald and her body burned and scarred. A typical step after a mastectomy is to have reconstructive surgery. To our surprise, the oncologist explained that Kristen was not a candidate for breast reconstruction because she was too thin and the skin was too parched to be stretched. David, as he always did, brought laughter to the difficult moment and claimed he had always loved "one-breasted women!"

I began to lose my emotions as the doctor spoke. Looking straight at Kristen, the doctor patted my knee in reassurance and said, "Hold on, Mom." I did manage to swallow my emotions until I said goodbye to Kristen and David near the elevators. I then ran to my car and cried out in anguish. I cried the entire 40-minute drive home. I had looked forward to the end of treatment. I had just assumed reconstructive surgery was the next step. I had longed for this nightmare interruption to end and to see both my daughter's body and her life put back together.

But, was it an interruption? Author Philip Yancey states,

> We have cut ourselves off from the stream of human history which has always accepted pain as an integral part of life. Until very recently, any balanced view of life had to account for pain as a normal, routine occurrence. Now it looms as the great intruder.[9]

I have to say that I was one of the many who saw Kristen's cancer as an intruder into our lives rather than an intricate piece of life's tapestry that would reshape and redefine our lives. Kristen's cancer was to be woven into the fabric of our entire family.

A positive bonus for Kristen came when her once straight hair began to grow back thick, dark, and wavy. She was determined that her life move forward and away from the stigma of cancer, and it surely did. Six weeks after treatment ended, in May, Kristen and David brought us a sonogram picture to announce they were going to have Baby Hartland!

I stood, frozen, in the kitchen as the sonogram was happily waved in my face. Within a nanosecond, I could sense a ping pong game playing in my brain! My inner thoughts were racing and reverberating, *Oh, no! No, you can't do this! What are you thinking? You just finished treatment...was this wise?* I was glad the thoughts remained inside! While the alarm bells rang throughout my brain, simultaneously, I smiled and said aloud to this dear, young couple, "You did do this...you are really going to have a baby!" I embraced the moment of celebration, and I embraced the happy couple who looked forward to their child. Soon, the entire Stone and Hartland families were rejoicing over the news. Incredibly, the due date for the baby was set for December 25! Miraculously, the Lord had preserved Kristen's ability to conceive.

At the June reassessment appointment to determine if Kristen still met the NED status, she informed her oncologist that she was pregnant. To protect the baby, all testing was canceled.

In July, Erica and Kristen spent a week together with their Nanny, John's mother, in New York. Norma had had a malignant tumor removed from her breast and was recovering. She was anxious and in need of reassurance. Kristen and her Nanny spent the week encouraging one another and comparing their injuries. A few weeks later, Erica came into Houston with her two little ones. We were celebrating that, just one year earlier, we were beginning chemotherapy but now treatment was done. We set out one day with Kristen to eat lunch together at La Madeleine's. Afterward, we had plans to go shopping.

In the parking lot after lunch, Kristen mentioned that her right shoulder hurt. During the ten-minute drive to the shopping center, her pain sharpened and escalated until she was doubled over and crying out in pain. I was concerned and urged Kristen to call her oncologist or at least consider a trip to the emergency room. In the shopping center parking lot, Kristen adamantly stated to me that she was done with cancer. She could not bring herself to call the oncologist. Instead, she called David, whose office was near the shopping center. He came immediately to take her home. She attributed the shoulder pain to carrying heavy bags through the airport during the recent trip to visit her grandmother.

The shoulder pain continued intermittently during the next few days. The following week, Kristen made an appointment with an orthopedist who suggested physical therapy for undetermined shoulder pain. At the appointment, I thought I might be able to enlist the doctor in an intervention. I looked directly at this orthopedist who had only a snapshot of the big picture and asked, "Do you think Kristen should call her oncologist?" I hoped he would somehow sense the urgency I was feeling and comprehend the questions behind my question. Surely, my eyes were sending the complete picture and surely his brain was downloading the pertinent details! I just knew that, between my serious question and the desperate, imploring look I was giving him, he would respond with wisdom and direction. His polite gaze immediately shifted away from me and to his patient, as he calmly said, "This is your choice."

I wanted to shake him like a tree! But, once again, what was I thinking? Although I sensed urgency, although the mother bear feelings were overpowering, I was powerless! Once again, I had to remind myself, mother power is gone when your child is 26 and married, no less! In my mind, I could see a new ministry being created from the entire year of choices made by my young, married daughter—the "Let It Go" ministry! Parents of adult children are to observe—

only observe. Support—only support. Love deeply, care for, pray for, cry over—but say nothing unless asked! I had tried to enlist persuasive wisdom from a doctor and I had failed in my quest.

Without any further questions or diagnostic tests, the orthopedic doctor prescribed physical therapy for Kristen's shoulder and off we went. Once again, I was grateful to be Kristen's driver, I was grateful to deliver her to therapy, but I knew all thoughts, all concerns, all misgivings had to stay tucked inside myself. Let. It. Go.

Kristen had decided to return to teaching. She and I spent a couple of days decorating and preparing her room at school. As we walked back and forth from the parking lot with boxes, Kristen was short of breath and commented that it was because of the pregnancy. I replied that it was unusual at five months of pregnancy to be this unusually fatigued and short of breath. Once again, I spoke; then I let it go and simply supported. I truly did support her desire for this young life growing within her. I knew this desire well. She longed for this young child to be born just as I had longed for her so many years before. I wanted this grandchild and many more, just as she and David had dreamed of and planned.

Our lives and schedules seemed to be smoothing out by September. John had started a new job September 1st. I was thrilled that I was back to teaching in the Woman's Bible study at church. I marvel at times when I grasp that God's plans for my journey here on earth are different than mine. I would never have woven cancer for my child into my journey, yet she had successfully navigated the treatment. I marveled that God had given me the strength to pass through that difficult year.

I believed now that the worst was behind us. That September, there was a sense of normalcy. Yet, God is an incomprehensible God and in our finite minds we sometimes cannot understand His ways.

After three weeks of teaching Bible Study, instead of preparing the next lecture, I was frantically searching through Mapquest to find Poteau, Oklahoma. John had been with friends on their annual motorcycle trip to the Ozarks. He slid his motorcycle into a cement wall and was in intensive care with blood in his lungs because of several broken ribs. My sister-in-law, Paula, and I drove nine hours to be with him. When we arrived, John gave us a drug-induced groggy smile and patted my hand. His injuries were not life-threatening, but he was in a lot of physical pain and would need to stay hospitalized for several days.

The day after I arrived in Poteau, Paula and I were returning from lunch when a nurse asked if either of us was Darla Stone. When I confirmed that I was, she told me that I had received a call from Kristen, who had asked that I call as soon as possible. With a sense of foreboding, I went to John's room and returned the call. Kristen told me that she had spent the morning in an emergency room because the combination of her shoulder pain and breathing difficulties had reached an intolerable level. Tests indicated that the cancer had returned with full force in her lungs and liver. The shoulder pain she had been experiencing during the last several weeks had been caused by her tumor-filled liver. The tumors enlarged the liver and it had begun pressing against the rib cage, which resulted in shoulder pain. The breathing difficulties were due to hundreds of small tumors in her lungs.

On the phone, Kristen admonished me, "Don't think about Jeff. I am not Jeff. I will get through this!" Jeff was a dear family friend who had died of liver cancer within two weeks of diagnosis. Kristen had obviously thought about Jeff when she was told about the tumors, and she knew my thoughts would run wild! She was obviously running the scenarios and reassuring herself, as well.

I stood in an Oklahoma hospital with John, yet I longed to be in the emergency room in Houston. John was hazy with painkillers and couldn't fully comprehend the situation. The emotions of both weekend events overwhelmed me. I was at the deepest point of sorrow that I had ever known. After the phone call, I left John's hospital room and walked blindly into a wall. A perceptive, compassionate nurse pulled me into a break room. She gently pulled me into her arms, held me tightly, and prayed, "Jesus, we need You now." Through my frantic sobs, I kept repeating, "I know Jesus will hold me." I never cried so hard and long in my life! It seemed to me that I wouldn't be able to bring my emotions under control. The nurse apparently thought the same and called John's doctor, who prescribed a pill that allowed my wild emotions to give way to blissful sleep.

When I woke up an hour later, I begged Paula to get me back to the hotel. I didn't want to be emotionally distraught and crying in a strange hospital. Back at the hotel, Paula held me and we cried and prayed together. The next morning, Paula and I flew back to Houston to be with Kristen while some dear friends drove to Poteau to be with John. A few days later, our friends drove him back to Houston because his collapsed lung prevented him from flying.

Chapter Seven

CHEMO...BABY...CHEMO

How unsearchable are God's judgments and unfathomable His ways!
Romans 11:33b

It was late September and we were back at MD Anderson. The scene was surreal. Erica and I sat in a conference room with David and his parents, plus several of his family members. Kristen and John sat side by side in wheel chairs. Kristen had been transferred to a new oncologist, who specialized in pregnant women with cancer. It was an extremely heart-wrenching meeting. The news was grim. We learned that the cancer had metastasized and had progressed to stage 4. I don't know who created this terminology of stages, but there is no number 5; the final stage of cancer is 4 and most often equates to terminal.

The specialist, Dr. Theriault, explained to us that he had spoken to several of his colleagues regarding Kristen's case.

His colleagues had advised that Kristen should deliver the baby immediately. Dr. Theriault told us that he disagreed with them. He gently told us that he did not believe that Kristen would be able to survive a c-section to deliver the baby.

The room grew profoundly quiet as we tried to grasp what he was saying. My child was sitting next to me, taking in breath, yet her death was imminent. He also stated that, if they chose to wait until the baby was born to begin chemo treatments, the fast-growing tumors would result in her death within two months. Her baby was not due for three months! It was difficult to fathom that death was so close for both Kristen and her unborn child.

Although I couldn't bear to hear more, I listened as Dr. Theriault continued relaying a course of action that he believed would be best. Because she could not safely deliver the baby, he advised that Kristen continue her pregnancy and begin treatment immediately. At this point, Kristen was beginning her third trimester. Dr. Theriault believed the baby was well formed and he believed that the placental wall would filter the harmful effects of the chemotherapy, keeping the baby safe. We placed our trust in his expertise.

The stage 4 diagnosis now qualified Kristen for the smart drug, Herceptin, that the FDA had been so reticent about approving. Dr. Theriault also prescribed a chemo drug to be added called Navelbine. The decision he made was medically untested and later proved to be of national medical significance. We left the conference room and went directly to the chemotherapy unit. The tremendous battle to keep both Kristen and her baby alive began that night.

Incredibly, the medicine was very effective and the tumors in her lungs began shrinking immediately! During the next several weeks, an army of volunteers prepared meals for Kristen and David. David took a leave of absence from work to support Kristen through this precarious time. I asked Kristen if she wanted me to resign from all volunteer help and women's ministry so that I could be available to her. She said yes. When she felt strong enough, Kristen and I returned to her classroom at school and packed up her personal items to make way for the new teacher.

Kristen's oncologist coordinated care with a high-risk obstetrician and appointments doubled. The obstetrician scheduled weekly ultrasounds to examine the baby. At some point, these were increased to twice a week. The amniotic fluid that is vital to a baby decreases when a mother is on chemo therapy, hence the ultrasounds. In addition to the chemo, Kristen was also taking pain medication. I was apprehensive about the baby's health, even though Dr. Theriault had reassured us. I thought the baby might come out with its head spinning from all the drugs.

In the midst of the crisis in which we found ourselves, Kristen was still glad to be carrying her child. She continued to look forward to being a mother. What else could we think to do between chemo treatments and ultrasounds except celebrate with a baby shower! The many friends and family who had gathered at our home for Kristen's wedding shower two years earlier joined us once again with hopeful expectation of the life Kristen carried. Onesies, activity mats, blankets, a boppy, and a baby swing rounded out the celebration. Kristen was radiant with joy for the child she carried.

Around that time, Kristen began a journal for her child. On November 13, she wrote,

> It's the middle of the night and I can't fall asleep. I am getting excited about teaching you to learn. (I am a school teacher.) I know you are going to be so smart. Your dad is very smart and loves to learn and we both love to read. I hope you love these things as much as we do. Today I had my chemotherapy treatment. I have it every Thursday. Your Nana and dad come with me—every time. Dad usually gets into things he's not supposed to. Today he got in a wheelchair and was doing wheelies.
>
> I am so thankful that God allowed me to be pregnant with you before I got cancer again. I always pray that He lets me live 'til I'm old, old, old so I can be your mom.

An ultrasound in mid-November indicated that the amniotic fluid had dried up completely at 35 weeks. An immediate decision was made to have Kristen induced into labor. We were all thanking God on November 18, 2003 when Samuel—the creation of love between my daughter and her precious husband, David—came into this world. In September, Kristen had been given two months to live. Almost two months to that very day, Samuel was born! They chose the name Samuel because they were inspired by Hannah's story in the Bible. Hannah had desperately prayed for a son. When he was born, she named him Samuel, explaining, "I have asked him of the Lord." As soon as the baby was born, a team of doctors literally swooped into the room and whisked Sam away to the neonatal unit of Texas Children's Hospital. Texas Children's Hospital is attached to St. Luke's Hospital where Kristen gave birth.

I left Kristen's room later and went to the NICU. A nurse allowed me to hold Sam, God's sweet gift of life, and I sat in a rocking chair gazing at this incredible miracle God had given us. Amazingly, after 24 hours, Sam was cleared from the neonatal unit in Texas Children's and sent back to the regular nursery in St. Luke's Hospital. Samuel was not affected by the drugs that his mother needed to survive. He experienced only severe reflux, as most preemies do, and he had a great set of screaming lungs, letting everyone know his tummy hurt!

God was faithful in forming the inward parts of Samuel, weaving them together inside the womb of his mother until the appointed time of his arrival. God gave us a sweet gift in the fact that Sam looks just like his mother. He has dark brown hair and his mother's big brown eyes, her face, and the same dimple on his cheek. Samuel will also grow to be like his daddy, David—tenderhearted, devoted to his family, protective over those he loves.

The day after Sam was born, Kristen was scheduled for her routine chemotherapy. We had been advised that, if we went through the proper channels and paper trails, Kristen would have to be discharged from St. Luke's Hospital in order to be taken to MD Anderson for her chemo treatment. In this massive medical center, St. Luke's just happens to be across the parking lot from MD Anderson. We were advised by an anonymous nurse that it might be simpler if we were just to take "a walk across the parking lot." So, after the morning rounds with visits from both doctors and shift nurses, David stayed in the room with the baby while Kristen and I went for "a walk."

As we left the hospital to cross the parking lot, I noted that it was a crisp and clear November day with an azure blue sky. The roses were still in full bloom just outside of MD Anderson—a beautiful day! In the midst of crisis, it is almost shocking to view vivid colors of red blossoms, green grass, blue sky, and bright, yellow sun. Senses are infused and normalcy is briefly noted—the sun has risen, the earth is still in place, and all is right with the world! We are simply stepping out for a walk! Of course, we both weren't walking; Kristen, who had just given birth, was in a wheelchair! I was in a surreal scene once again, pushing my child quickly across a parking lot from one hospital to the other so that she could receive chemo! Thankfully, the treatment went without a hitch. Within two hours, Kristen was back in her hospital bed with her newborn in her arms.

Chapter Eight

A WIFE AND A MOM

No mountain, no valley
no gain or loss we know
could keep us from Your love.

How high, how wide
no matter where I am
healing is in Your hands.
How deep, how strong
and now by Your grace I stand
healing is in Your hands.[10]

Six weeks later, Christmas came once again and we all celebrated together. Everyone was rejoicing because Samuel was healthy—my child, however, still battled courageously for her life. Weekly chemo treatments continued. At least three days each week, I would drive the 40 minutes to pick Kristen and Sam up and bring them home to spend the day. I was just as glad for this task as I had been years earlier driving to all of her track meets and practices. It was a privilege to be her mom and caregiver six hours each of those days. I would care for Sam while Kristen rested. I delighted in holding Sam against me as he slept, just as I had once held his mother.

On January 20, Kristen wrote in Sam's journal,

> I love your smile. Your eyes light up and your mouth gives the biggest smile! On Monday the 12th, we got the best news from my doctor about the results of my MRI and chest x-ray. I was so nervous going in, thinking that it was going to be bad news. Then he said there was almost complete resolution of all the metastases. It's almost all gone! We were so happy and thankful. What a miracle! God has given me more time here on earth to be your mom!

One spring day, Kristen and I went to lunch, with Sam in his infant carrier. It felt so normal! Kristen and David were thinking of moving out of their rental loft, and we had fun brainstorming where they might live. As we were talking that day, Kristen shared that she had heard of a three-year-old child with cancer. She told me that if that were Sam, she would just want to die with him. I answered, "You are finally able to understand what I feel as your mom! You know the deep well of a mother's love for her child! You know what the 'mother bear syndrome' feels like!" Later, as we approached the car, she touched my shoulder and said, "You can't have thoughts like dying too. Mom, you have to be there for Sam." Her words sharply etched themselves into the core of my being. We had never gone to that depth before—spoken of the possibility that Kristen would not be raising her child. The moment was brief and painful and one that is forever etched in my mind. We quickly shifted our focus back to neighborhoods where this young couple could live and raise their family.

The smart drug plus other chemo reduced Kristen's tumors for about six months and then quit working. For research purposes, Kristen—and many other test cases like hers—were able to prove that Herceptin needs to be given at the first diagnosis in order to be most effective. FDA has now approved this and women are living full lives because of the research in which Kristen participated. In 2004, however, Herceptin came too late for those in Stage 4.

Several tumors continued to grow in Kristen's liver and, in April, she began a different type of chemo, Xeloda, which was a tablet taken orally. Her thick, dark brown, wavy hair was gone once again. The tumors again reduced in size for a time, but this new chemo worked for only a few months. By August 2004, there were two tumors that maintained their size and presence in Kristen's liver. The Xeloda dosage was increased but was still ineffective.

Wanting to encourage Kristen and David, someone in the family came up with of the idea of secretly raising funds for a vacation trip. Both David's family and ours, along with a few friends, enthusiastically pooled money together, all unbeknownst to Kristen and David. On David's birthday that year, the two families gathered at our house, eagerly anticipating the surprise. David opened the gift and they were both surprised by and excited about the vacation trip. Within a few weeks, between doctor appointments, they were off to

Cabo San Lucas for a relaxing getaway. It was fun for John and me too, as we were Sam's babysitters for the week. Kristen wrote in Sam's journal,

> On Wednesday, July 21, you woke up saying "Mama." I was so excited to hear you say that. You played all day and repeated it over and over. When you get real sad and cry you will say it, also. You lift up your arms for me to pick you up. We have the rocking chair in your room now and I rock you a lot. I love all our moments together.
>
> We went to Cabo for a trip on August 6, your dad and me. We missed you so much. I slept with your blue blankie and called home twice to see how you were doing. When Nana and you and Rebecca picked us up from the airport, you looked at us and then you started to laugh and smile. When we left you were just getting your first top tooth and now your second top tooth is coming in!

Kristen had stood firmly in her conviction, throughout two years of treatment, to not be identified with cancer. She wanted to simply be known as a wife to David and, when Sam came, a mother to her baby boy. Yet, that summer and fall, a few events occurred that began to create a shift in her views.

In July, she heard of a photographer who was taking photos of cancer-surviving moms with their children. We drove for an hour or so to have the pictures taken. The photographer, Alisa Murray, planned to create a calendar highlighting each mom. She stated that the calendar would be sold at the Susan G. Komen Run for the Cure Race. In Houston, this annual event is held in October and has raised millions of dollars for breast cancer research. Ms. Murray mentioned that she would choose twelve moms, so we had no idea if Kristen would be chosen.

A second indication of a shift in Kristen's long-held convictions occurred in September. Kristen was invited to a dinner sponsored by the Young Survival Coalition. The YSC mission statement reads that it "is an organization dedicated to the critical issues unique to young women who are diagnosed with breast cancer. It offers resources and connections so women feel supported." When she was invited, Kristen's first thought was to turn down the invitation. With some hesitance, she finally agreed to attend the event. The YSC statement proved to be true. It had been one year since Kristen had received the Stage 4 diagnosis. She found other young women with cancer, like herself, and began to feel a kinship through the site's online support posts.

In October, Kristen and I walked the Komen 5K event with Sam in his stroller. It was a sea of thousands of women running, walking, and in wheelchairs. At the end of the course, dozens of booths were set up with vendors selling their wares. We found Alisa Murray's calendar booth and we were pleasantly surprised. Kristen and Sam were chosen for January's picture! A quote Kristen had given read, "My cancer metastasized when I was six months pregnant. Every day I look into the eyes of my son, Sam, and see a miracle. My faith in Christ and the many prayers of His people make every day a victory!"

(1) Graduation Day, December, 2000; (2) Wedding Dance, February, 2001;
(3) Austin, 2001; (4) Christmas after chemo, 2002;
(5) Sam is born, November, 2003

(6) A mom holds her son, Winter, 2004; (7) Hiking near the Guadalupe River, Winter, 2004; (8) Cabo San Lucas, Summer, 2004; (9) Christmas Card, December, 2004; (10) Sam and Kristen, Winter, 2005

Chapter Nine

ONE FINAL CHRISTMAS

I'm waiting, I'm waiting on You Lord
And I am hopeful, I'm waiting on You Lord
Though it is painful, but patiently I will wait

I'm waiting, I'm waiting on You Lord
And I am peaceful, I'm waiting on You Lord
Though it's not easy no, but faithfully I will wait
Yes, I will wait

While I'm waiting I will serve You
While I'm waiting I will worship
While I'm waiting I will not faint
I'll be running the race even while I wait.[11]

Kristen looked forward to all the firsts that Sam experienced: sitting, crawling, standing, and walking. She was there for his first smile and his first tooth. She was able to cherish the sound of his voice saying, "Ma." In November, she prepared and hosted a fun-filled first birthday party for Sam with friends and family. Later in Sam's journal, Kristen wrote,

> Wow! You are ONE! I can't believe a whole year has gone by. On your birthday, Daddy and I went into your room with the video camera and sang 'Happy Birthday.' I sang it to you all day long. About 40 people came for your party. Daddy bought so many decorations, food and drinks. I made lots of cupcakes. I opened all your gifts for you. You still don't know how to rip off wrapping paper.
>
> I have loved and will always cherish our first year with you. You have grown so much. I love to watch you discover the world. You are the light of my life. I love you, Sam!

As she cherished Sam's firsts, the tumors continuously grew in her liver, which caused Kristen to feel weak. In October, the oncologist switched medications yet again. A new, experimental chemotherapy called GM-CSF was given to her. Unfortunately, by December, this experimental drug was proven to be ineffective. Kristen's oncologist then chose to try a combination of Herceptin, Taxotere, and Carboplatin. I had to face the reality that Kristen would be connected to chemo and continued assaults to her physical body for the rest of her life.

On December 20, I heard that Kristen and David would be out for the evening. John and I picked up a Christmas tree. Along with John's sister, Sherry, and her family, like little elves, we decorated their home. We packed away the empty boxes and left, imagining their response. Later, as they pulled into the driveway, Kristen saw the lights first and screamed, and David hit the brakes, suspecting disaster! She told me later that she had decided not to decorate because she didn't have the strength to prepare for Christmas, so they were very pleasantly surprised.

Christmas was a sweet celebration with all of our family gathering together. Erica, her husband Jonathan, and three little ones—Nathan, Megan, and Andrew; plus our other two children, Carl and Rebecca, along with Kristen, David and Sam! A sweet gift from God was a Christmas Eve snowfall. In Houston, Texas, perhaps an inch of snow may fall once every decade. This particular night it snowed heavy, wet flakes that stayed for a time. I grew up in snow country and have always missed it in Houston's winters. Happy memories of snow-filled Christmases from our years in Chicago came to us all that night.

After Christmas, Kristen wrote to Sam once again,

> I love you so much that my heart squeezes and I can't breathe. My love for you is so great that I can't even explain it all. If I love you that much—and I am just a fallen, sinful human being—then think about how much and how perfectly God loves you, Sam. He is your Creator and He is always looking out for your good.

During that time, I began to feel like Abraham taking his son to Mt. Moriah. The Bible relates the life story of Abraham in the book of Genesis. He was called by God, just as we all are. Abraham responded in faith and believed God's promises. One of those promises was that he would have descendants through his son, Isaac. A confusing command from God came to Abraham when Isaac was a young boy. God commanded Abraham to sacrifice Isaac as a burnt offering. I could imagine Abraham's conflicted feelings as he walked slowly along willing to obey God, yet, with his child at his side, dreading the enormity of loss.

Abraham was willing to obey God when life did not make sense. Abraham's obedience was rewarded by God. God provided a different sacrifice, a ram, in place of Isaac. It seemed that I was walking my own dear child up a treacherous mountain path to an awaiting altar, hoping against all hope that God might allow the same outcome for me as He did for Abraham. I prayed God would make a way that Kristen would live—please, please make a way!

During all of this, I prayed these words to God from Psalm 130:1, "Out of the depths I have cried to Thee, O Lord. Lord, hear my voice! Let Thine ears be attentive to the voice of my supplications." I continued to sense that I was waiting upon the Lord. Psalm 130:5-6 goes on to say, "I wait for the Lord, my soul does wait and in His word do I hope. My soul waits for the Lord, more than the watchmen for the morning—indeed more than the watchmen for the morning." I thanked God with a grateful heart that He heard my cry and the gift of time was given to all of us. None of us know the measure of our days, but we can count each given moment and day spent with family as a treasure to bury deep in the heart. I placed precious single moments of time into my treasure box.

The combination drugs that were started in December were mildly successful for two months and then failed. The liver tumors were increasing in size once again. Since the onset of Kristen's cancer, an arsenal of eight different chemotherapy drugs had been prescribed. All had failed. Due to this failure, in March 2005, the oncologist ordered whole body scans and MRI's.

The words of the first doctor that we had spoken with nearly three years earlier were proven to be true. Kristen did have the most aggressive form of breast cancer. The unrelenting, insidious cancer had made its way to the bone in her spine. Worse than that, however, several malignant tumors were found in Kristen's brain.

We were told that the brain took priority and treatment focus had to shift. For over a year, the battle had focused on the tumors in her liver, yet that treatment had to be stopped immediately. One battle had to cease while a new, deadlier battle was waged. Kristen began a ten-day whole-brain radiation. The inch of her new hair growth was burned and came out in clumps. Her face broke out into red welts and rashes, and she began to wear ear plugs because every sound was painfully amplified. I recalled how devastated a family feels when one tumor is discovered in a loved one. Kristen had several! In the brain! Could any place in her body be left untouched by this cancer?

Early in May, ten days after the brain radiation ended, the treatment focus returned to Kristen's liver. The liver had become greatly enlarged, due to the fact that the two large tumors had now formed into one large tumor that filled 85 percent of her liver. Kristen's oncologist sent her to a liver oncologist who suggested a radical treatment called Hepatic Arterial Infusion. The plan was for two infusions to be done one month apart.

Extreme situations call for extreme measures. Hepatic Arterial Infusion delivers a chemotherapy (in this case, Cisplatin) through a catheter placed in her hepatic artery and directly onto the liver. The goal of this treatment is to flood the tumor with a chemo wash. The risk for Kristen was that the 15 percent of functioning liver might be destroyed. Simultaneously, Kristen was to receive a second chemo, Doxyrubicin, through her port-a-cath. The treatment took just two hours, yet Kristen had to stay in the hospital for seven days because the side effects were more severe than she had experienced with the other drugs she had received in the three years of treatment.

Kristen did experience a sweet moment in the midst of her hospital stay, though. On Mother's Day, David took Sam to the hospital to visit his mom. John, Rebecca, and I stayed with Sam in a lobby waiting room while David went to get Kristen. She was able to be wheeled down to celebrate Mother's Day with her son. Sam, oblivious to his surroundings, was just happy to see his mom. He handed Kristen his gift and played all around her, fascinated by the wheels of the chair.

Chapter Ten

A MOTHER LOVES HER SON

Even though I walk through the valley
of the shadow of death
Your perfect love is casting out fear.

And even when I'm caught in the middle
of the storms of this life
I won't turn back,
I know You are near

And I will fear no evil
for my God is with me.
And, if my God is with me,
whom then shall I fear? [12]

Throughout Kristen's physical deterioration during the month of May, she continued to be a mother to her young son. When she still had strength enough to walk with the help of a cane, she would take Sam to the park across the street from their home. We have a picture of her laying on the couch, when she was without physical strength, smiling at Sam as he happily played by her side.

Knowing Kristen had experienced a radical treatment, out-of-town friends came in for a weekend visit to offer encouragement. While Kristen napped, David, Sam, and their friends went swimming. Sam fell and cried at the pool. They searched him over, couldn't find anything wrong, and continued playing with him. When they arrived home, Kristen looked at Sam and said, "What happened to his tooth? It's chipped!" Most mothers know their child's blueprint inside and out, and Kristen was no different. With one look at her child, she knew what was missing. She loved being the mother of Sam.

Later that evening, David and their friends sat together in the living room talking while Kristen slept. They were surprised when she walked into the room with her Bible, (The Message Bible) telling them to listen to her as she read from Job 42:

> I'm convinced. You can do anything and everything. Nothing and no one can upset Your plans. You asked, 'Who is this muddying the water, ignorantly confusing the issue, second-guessing my purposes?' I admit it. I was the one. I babbled on about things far beyond me, made small talk about wonders way over my head. You told me, 'Listen, and let me do the talking. Let me ask the questions. You give the answers.' I

admit I once lived by rumors of You, now I
have it all firsthand—from my own eyes and
ears! I'm sorry—forgive me. I'll never do that
again, I promise! I'll never again live on crusts
of hearsay, crumbs of rumor.

Kristen then animatedly shared that she, too, knew God
firsthand with her own eyes and ears. Although her body was
weakening, her spirit was gaining strength as she grew closer
to God.

Since the first infusion, Kristen had gone from walking
with a cane to riding in a wheelchair in her ever weakening
condition. It increasingly became difficult to keep food
down. When the day came in early June to discuss the second
infusion with the liver oncologist, he delivered grave news
to us. The first infusion had not worked; the 15 percent of
functioning liver had been negatively affected and was failing.
There would not be a second infusion. Instead, we were told
to set an appointment with Kristen's regular oncologist, Dr.
Theriault.

On Friday, June 3, we met with Kristen's oncologist and
heard the unbearable words, "We have done all we can do
and it is time to call hospice." David responded in disbelief,
questioning the doctor and saying that there must surely be
other options. Kristen, David's mother Joan, and I cried quietly.
Hospice—not a word that anyone wants to use or need. The
word sounded foreign and unbearable to my ears. David asked
the doctor if there would be time enough to travel. The doctor
responded that there may be six weeks. Six weeks of precious
moments to grasp. Six weeks of tender words to remember.

David and Kristen wanted a weekend of their own before calling hospice. David's family and close friends gathered. Erica and Jonathan drove in from San Antonio and visited with them Saturday evening. On Sunday, Kristen asked that I visit along with John's sister, Paula. I immediately jumped in the car! I warmed up chicken broth in an attempt to give her nourishment.

A psalmist once wrote, "My heart is in anguish within me, and the terrors of death have fallen upon me. Fear and trembling come upon me, and horror has overwhelmed me" (Psalm 55:4-5). These words from 3,000 years ago succinctly spoke the condition of my being. In the silence of night, I became filled with extreme anxiety and scattered, torturous, frightening thoughts. I became gripped with fear as if my firm hold for belief and truth were in question. I cried out into the darkness, "I do believe in Jesus Christ. He is my Lord and Savior. I will believe this to be truth." I then had clarity of thought regarding the stark reality of my deepest fear. I said to my Savior, "You're going to take her home, aren't You?" I immediately felt that quiet, inner response from Jesus. He said, "I am." Then I cried, "You are going to have to do more than hold me in the palm of Your hand; You will have to wrap Your arms around me and wrap me like a cocoon so I can do this." I then heard in my spirit, "I will."

The thought of Kristen leaving this earth was breaking my heart, yet, I processed the thoughts further. For many years, I had proclaimed that I loved Jesus. I had professed that Jesus was in control of my life and that I trusted Him. Now, the One I loved and trusted most was going to take my child—a piece of my heart—to Heaven to be with Him. How could I not trust Him in this, as well?

That Monday morning, three days after hearing the unbearable word, hospice, spoken, I stayed home so Erica could have some time alone with her sister. Erica gave Kristen a pedicure and painted her nails as they visited. Later that morning, the doctor called David to relay that the latest blood test indicated that Kristen's organs were actively shutting down. He said there was no need to force her to eat or drink. He told David that Kristen would not live a few more weeks as we had hoped, but rather, just a few more days. The promise of six weeks was gone. David decided it was time to make the call to hospice.

When Kristen woke from a nap, she asked to be taken to the couch so she would be able to hold Sam. David and Erica sat on either side of her, as David relayed the news that they didn't have as long as they thought they would have. Both David and Erica began to cry. Kristen put an arm around each and held them as they cried. She had begun her transition from the earthly bonds of this life into new life. As she looked forward, she could comfort those who would be left behind.

Although Kristen was transitioning and would sleep deeply for hours at a time, she continued being Sam's mom. A week before, a prescription for vitamins had been given to the pharmacy for Sam. Now, several times, she would wake out of a deep sleep and say to David, "Sam, Walgreens." At first, David thought she wasn't making any sense. When the automated reminder call from Walgreens finally came a few days later, we knew Kristen's nurturing for Sam had never stopped.

The next morning, Sam, full of energy, climbed onto Kristen's bed to play and snuggle with his mom. Kristen woke briefly and could sense the movement by her side. She asked Erica what the movement was; and, when she heard it was Sam, she turned toward him and began stroking his back. Incredibly, Sam snuggled closer to her side and fell asleep with her—a rarity for an active eighteen month old. It was that ordinary snuggling moment that became Kristen's final touch of love for, and from, her son. Sam's snuggle was a sweet gift of love to his mother.

The small house filled with family and friends throughout the day. Hospice delivered some equipment and left. I was glad they left because I didn't want the intrusion of a stranger when time was so precious. Ever attentive, David sat close to Kristen, holding her hand. John and Erica sat at the opposite side of the bed. A few of David's sisters also gathered around the bed, while his other sisters were playing with Sam and greeting friends who came. His sister, Jill, is a nurse and she helped with the equipment. She gave us great encouragement with her presence.

I sat near the bottom of the big king-sized bed, holding Kristen's other hand as she slept. I treasured the moment, noting a small scar from some long forgotten childhood fall. I spent time looking at the dear, sweet face I had loved for so long. I cherished each feature of her face and each breath she took.

I will always be grateful that I was with Kristen when she took her last breath, just as I was there for her very first breath. She went to be with Jesus on Tuesday afternoon, June 7, 2005. She was at home in her bed as those who loved her most on this earth saw her take her last breath.

And I will fear no evil
for my God is with me.
And, if my God is with me,
whom then shall I fear?

Oh, no, You never let go
through the calm and through the storm
Oh, no, You never let go
in every high and every low.
Oh, no, You never let go of me.
Lord, you never let go of me.[13]

Chapter Eleven

FREE FALL INTO THE VALLEY OF THE SHADOW

Heaven is the face of a little girl
with dark brown eyes that disappear when she smiles
...God I know it's all this and so much more
But God, You know that it is what I'm aching for
God, You know I just can't see beyond the door.

Oh God, I know it's so much more than I can dream
It's far beyond anything I can conceive
So God, You know I'm trusting you until I see
Heaven in the face of my little girl.[14]

K risten was gone. For three years, I had sensed that I had been walking my child up a treacherous mountain path to an awaiting altar, but, unlike how God had dealt with Abraham, He had taken my Isaac. A blanket of unspeakable dread draped itself over me. The dread was a deep fear of my own grief. I didn't know this grief, and it frightened me to the core. I couldn't measure the length of it. I couldn't research the depths and the side edges. I might just be lost there and not ever return whole. I could sense that I was already beginning to buckle inwardly, collapsing beneath the weight of this unknown dread.

Incredibly, I found an author who had also experienced similar thoughts as I had regarding Abraham. In 1974, after the death of his daughter, John Claypool wrote,

> I know something of the overwhelming shock that Abraham must have experienced when he realized one night that God was demanding his son of him. There is no way to describe the mixture of horror and bitterness and terror and fear that churns up within one at the advent of such a realization...Abraham got to go down the mountain with his child by his side...But my situation is different. Here I am, left alone on that mountain...and the question is: how on earth do I get down and move back to the normalcy of life again? I am left to grope through the darkness by myself and to ask: "where do I go from here? Is there a road out, and if so, which one?"[15]

When a child dies, a parent undergoes a rapid free fall into the valley of the shadow of death. Whether through tragic accident, suicide, or prolonged illness, such as Kristen's, the descent into the valley is a radical plunge. I took a headlong dive into the solitary, expansive valley of grief. To me, the valley appeared to be bleak and sunless—I realized I was inside the shadow that death had created. This was a place that I could not possibly traverse. I did not wish to be inside the shadow but I could see no way out.

Psalm 23 states, "Yea, though I walk through the valley of the shadow of death, I will fear no evil, for Thou art with me." The key word in this sentence is *through*. I could not see any point in time when I would be walking through this valley and out again. The blanket of dread and darkness gripped me. I had no strength to move back into the sun.

I trusted Jesus completely, but this unknown darkness was untested. Could I be experiencing such unbearable fear and still have faith? I knew that the most repeated command in the Bible is "do not fear." For God to repeat this so often, He must know that fear is a strong emotion to defeat. He must know it can be a fierce, gripping force coming against us—a force that could trap and end any movement forward.

David's words of Psalm 61 were my sentiments: "Hear my cry, O God; give heed to my prayer. From the end of the earth I call to Thee, when my heart is faint; lead me to the rock that is higher than I. For Thou hast been a refuge for me, a tower of strength against the enemy."

I could visualize King David writing and crying as he wrote those words. I could see the flood waters and the imminent loss of strength that would lead to my own drowning. I knew the rock he wrote of, the one that was just a little higher and beyond my reach. I cried out, "God, I am trapped in dread and darkness. Please, Lord, please pull me up to the rock that is higher than this sadness, higher than my fear! I just need to rest and breathe for a moment under the weight of this burden."

Humans do experience fear in varying degrees—even those who wholeheartedly place their trust in God. David acknowledged his fear; he described it in detail in the psalm. He laid bare the truth. Then he turned his face to God. Just as he fully described his despair, his very next thought was written: "For Thou hast been a refuge for me, a tower of strength against the enemy." Many of his psalms begin with his cries. Those same psalms end with praise. Psalm 28 states,

> To You, O Lord, I call: my rock, do not be
> deaf to me, for if You are silent to me, I will
> become like those who go down to the pit.
> Hear the voice of my supplications….The
> Lord is my strength and my shield; my heart
> trusts in Him and I am helped; therefore my
> heart exults, and with my soul I shall thank
> Him.

In my deepest dread, Jesus did not leave me nor forsake me, just as had He promised in Hebrews 13:5. I leaned into Him and cried—a lot. I felt His strength and comfort. Together, Jesus and I began the slow journey through the expansive valley of the shadow.

God is our strength right in the unknown place of dread. He doesn't want us to fear, but He won't leave us or forsake us when we do. I knew that perfect love casts out fear. I continually recalled my request to God to cocoon me. Psalm 27:5 held my thoughts:

For in the day of trouble He will conceal me
in His tabernacle; in the secret place of His
tent He will hide me; He will lift me up on
a rock.

Slowly, I began to absorb the grief of Kristen's cancer and her final days. I was reeling from the shock of her death, yet I had also endured three years of emotional trauma and ongoing crises. There was very little time to process one incident before the next crisis occurred. I had been racing to appointments in the car, or taking care of Kristen and Sam, or spending long days at MD Anderson; and now, the urgency had come to an abrupt halt. In the quiet, I began to process the chaos of the past three years.

When I woke in the morning, my first conscious thought would be about Kristen. I would face the day with a groan as the ever-present dread fell upon me. When all was quiet at night, my last conscious thoughts were about Kristen. I began to pray that this dark passage would be redeemed and that Kristen's death would not remain void. I prayed that something profitable would come out of this suffering and loss.

I continued to process through my dreams, and I would cry in the morning as any given dream replayed in my mind. Kristen's age range would vary in my dreams from very young through being a teenager and on to being the beautiful woman that she became. In one particular dream, she was very young, 5 or 6, and her hair was long as it had been then. She didn't feel well and she walked up to me and raised her arms. I remember thinking, she has cancer, she's small, she will let me

79

hold her and comfort her. In another dream, I found Kristen sitting on a chair. I looked for David and Sam and then I could hear them playing behind a closed door. I placed my arms around her and began to carry her. She was very light and I could feel her long beautiful hair brush against my shoulder. (When she died, her hair was permanently gone due to the brain radiation.)

As my dream continued, I sang the chorus of an old hymn: "When we all get to Heaven, what a day of rejoicing that will be; when we all see Jesus, we'll sing and shout the victory!"[16] It was incredible that my mind could ponder and look forward to God's promise in my sleep. He promises that those who believe in Jesus Christ will one day shout the victory that we have passed through death into new life. It was also amusing both in the fact that the words were accurate and that I sang them clearly and on key!

Throughout Kristen's journey, I had wanted to see myself as a strong support but had felt myself to be weak. I had longed to comfort Kristen all the way through her pain, and I do believe that my presence in her life did encourage her. However, I could see that the main source of her earthly comfort was her husband, David. Kristen gained strength from David. If enduring love could cure cancer, then David's love would surely have cured Kristen. He was both strong and gentle in his love for Kristen. Just as John and I had cheered Kristen on at high school running events, David was the cheerleader in her final race. With the thoughts of God redeeming the dark passage, I began to pray for David—that God would hold him close and give him strength. I prayed he would not become bitter, but live righteously and without compromise.

A week after Kristen died, I asked David if we could intentionally set one day a week that Sam could spend with us. I had been helping Kristen care for Sam so much during the past year; and I knew if I left his life abruptly as well, he would feel an additional, unnecessary loss. It was agreed that Sam would spend each Friday night with us. We all benefited from the arrangement. David would have a parenting night off, and we would see Sam. John and I would have the opportunity to nurture our grandson.

David's birthday is June 30, three weeks after Kristen's death. The day before his birthday, he found a card Kristen had written to him. Some time after David found the card, he called me, crying. I mentioned to him that the timing of finding it was a perfect birthday present from Kristen. He shared some of what was written with us:

My Dearest David,

I love you more every day as you help me through these difficult and painful days. I believe God has prepared us for these moments. Your love for me is modeled after Christ's love for me. I know that God's love for us will carry us through these painful days. God has never asked us to understand and get over it. He wants to be the one we go to in our grief and in our weeping and in our remembering of our joyful day which will come again.

The greatest blessing Christ has given to you and me is Samuel Stone Hartland. He is our legacy and he will always be our miracle...Sam is another chord God has linked us together with, one that will never be broken...I know I have said it over a hundred times: no one should ever make you doubt that you are an amazing dad. I really believe it is a gift from God...

We will still pray every day for a miracle, but if God does not give us one, it doesn't change a single thing. His love is still the same, our love is still the same, and our love for Sam is still the same. Never question those things; they are true.

I love you with all I am; heart, soul, and body. Kristen

Chapter Twelve

TREASURES IN THE DARKNESS

I'm Alive
Even though a part of me has died
You take my heart and breathe it back to life
I've fallen into your arms open wide
When the hurt and the healer collide

Breathe
Sometimes I feel it's all that I can do
Pain so deep I can hardly move
Just keep my eyes completely fixed on you
Lord, take hold; pull me through.[17]

God hears us when we pray. We are told in James 5:16 that "the effective prayer of a righteous man can accomplish much." It was extremely difficult to wrap my mind around the fact that, when God answered my prayer, He said "No." Hundreds had prayed fervently for three years.

God answered in a way that was difficult for all who knew her. It was unfathomable to me that God gave Kristen to us, that He allowed her to walk this earth for 28 years and then chose to take her home. I could not comprehend this way of God. I came to realize that to search for comprehension would be too difficult a task.

Because I live on this side of heaven, my finite mind might not ever be able to grasp the plan of my infinite God. So, even though I couldn't wrap my mind around the *No*, I continued to trust Him. God's *No* became a settled matter in my heart. I did not see it as a betrayal or punishment from God. I did not see it as a misstep on my part to pray a better prayer to be heard by God. God's *No* did not change the fact that He loves me with an everlasting love. It did not change the fact that I love Him in return.

However, life inside the shadow is a severe day-by-day reality. God chose to take Kristen to Heaven and that was my reality. Joni Eareckson Tada and Steven Estes wrote a book exploring suffering. I agreed wholeheartedly with their thoughts. They state,

> God's plan is specific...He screens the trials that come to each of us—These trials aren't evenly distributed from person to person. This can discourage us, for we are not privy to His reasons. But in God's wisdom and love, every trial in a Christian's life is ordained from eternity past, custom-made for that believer's eternal good, even when it doesn't seem like it.

God clearly claims to run the world—not "could" run it if He wanted to or "can" step in when He has to, but **does** run it—all the time. God claims that nothing touches us without first receiving His nod and that "all the days ordained for me were written in His book before one of them came to be" (Psalm 139:16). He says without blushing, "Is it not from the mouth of the Most High that both calamities and good things come?" (Lamentations 3:38).[18]

God is sovereign; His thoughts are not my thoughts, and His ways are not my ways. My way, of course, would be to have Kristen walking with us, loving David and raising Sam. But God is sovereign. I truly believed and rested in the fact that God had a far greater reason, beyond my comprehension, to take Kristen to Heaven.

Yet, simultaneously, my heart was in a constant aching mode and my grief was ever present, overwhelming my thoughts. The blanket of dread was weighty. From Psalm 56:8, King David wrote, "Put my tears in Thy bottle; are they not in Thy book?" I believe I cried enough tears to fill gallons of God's bottles. At times, I doubted I would ever walk out of the shadow of death and back into the light of a new day. I was seriously concerned that I might not ever be whole in mind again. Tada and Estes write,

> Suffering has not only rocked the boat, it has capsized it. We need assurance that the world

is not splitting apart at the seams. We need to know we aren't going to fizzle into a zillion atomic particles and go spinning off in space. We need to be reassured that the world, the universe, is not in nightmarish chaos, but orderly and stable. God must be at the center of things. He must be in the center of our suffering. What's more, He must be Daddy. Personal and compassionate. This is our cry.[19]

In this turmoil, I would beg my Father God to let me go home! I had always looked forward to my heavenly home, but at this point in my life, I **longed** to be there! I longed for the day that Jesus would set all things right and there would be no more physical breaks from love. This intense longing permeated my thoughts for months.

This longing did not mean I was suicidal. It did not mean that my faith was faltering. I simply did not want to continue this journey of grief; each day was agonizing and beyond my ability to traverse. I didn't want to be on this side of heaven; I wanted to be home with my Savior, the place of "no more pain" where my daughter now lived.

I wrote in my journal,

Isaiah says you will give me "treasures of darkness...in order that I may know it is You, the Lord, the God of Israel, who calls me by my name." I know that You have given me the treasures of darkness as You have led me through the valley of the shadow of death.

You have held me and allowed me to grieve.
You have spoken to me of Your everlasting
love in the deepest darkness of my pain. You
are Sovereign and I cannot comprehend Your
ways. I can only be held by You and rest
in You. It is darker than I could have ever
imagined and I cannot bear this grief alone.
Please, I pray, keep me ever mindful of the
treasures of darkness, and yet restore my
spirit in You.

We had two treasures in the darkness for which we
marveled. The first began five months before Kristen died.
The company John worked for was purchased and the new
firm eliminated his division. John was without a job, yet he
was given a good severance package. For the next five months,
John searched for a new position. This treasure was that John's
hectic schedule was abruptly freed up so that he was able to
spend quality time with Kristen during her final months of
life. Ten days before she died, Kristen called us around 5:30
in the morning. She had been experiencing insomnia and
told us she had been praying all night for John to get a return
call that he had been expecting from a potential employer.
With confidence, Kristen said, "Dad, you will get the call this
morning!" Four hours later, John received the call and was
hired!

The second incredible treasure in the darkness was
personally affirming to me. A week before Kristen died,
David had created a website to keep friends informed of her
progress. Through the website, after her death, guests began

leaving messages beyond our imagination. We began to see a marked pattern of a legacy that Kristen left behind. At some point during the final year of her life, she had joined an online support group for young women with breast cancer. Just a few of the many amazing and encouraging comments follow:

> Kristen's log-in name was Hart Shine and never was there a more appropriate name. She inspired us and made us laugh. She supported us and she gave us the greatest honor and gift; she shared her journey. She has touched each of us in a deep and profound way. — anonymous

> I am also a stage 4 cancer survivor. Kristen reached out to me when I had no strength and encouraged me. I thank God for having brought her into my life. — Jeni

> She was one of the most selfless people I have had the privilege of communicating with. She was down to earth, loving, never bitter, never preachy. — Ella

> She blessed me with her encouragement when I was diagnosed. She helped me achieve a sense of peace. — Cheryl

> We cherished her...she made a great impact on me. She had a peace about her. — anonymous

I was especially touched because, as her mother, I had held onto a concern throughout Kristen's cancer journey. I voiced it to her on several occasions. I wanted to know that she was processing and verbalizing to someone—anyone— her thoughts and feelings of this difficult passage. Each time I brought this up, she would assure me that she spoke with David. Yet, because she would not share her thoughts with me, I was concerned that she still might be overburdened.

The words of these young cancer survivors were very personal treasures in the darkness of my grief. They had no idea that they were imparting a sense of Kristen's well-being to me. I was so grateful to know that Kristen was processing and communicating with many. I thanked God that the women could sense a peace in Kristen. I thanked God for allowing me to catch a glimpse of Kristen's heart and legacy she left to these young women.

Chapter Thirteen

FILLING THE VOID

We had so many plans for you
We had so many dreams
And now you've gone away
and left us with the memories of your smile
and nothing we can say
and nothing we can do
can take away the pain
the pain of losing you, but...

We can cry with hope
We can say goodbye with hope,
cause we know our goodbye is not the end, oh no
And we grieve with hope
cause we believe with hope
there's a place by God's grace,
there's a place where we'll see your face again
We'll see your face again.[20]

S oon after Kristen died, a friend shared her own journey of grief with me. Her seventeen-year-old daughter, infused with life, walked out of the house one afternoon to see a friend. Her car missed a curve in the road and, within the hour, she was gone. My friend had gone before me into the bleak, sunless shadow of death and—years later—she helped me know what to expect. She told me that, after her daughter died, she had an intense need for sleep. What a relief to get this permission to rest! I forced myself to follow through on one or two daily tasks and then each afternoon for weeks, I could be found wrapped in my red throw—the same throw that used to be wrapped around Kristen—asleep on the couch. Once again, a Psalmist conveyed my thoughts, "For in the day of trouble, He will conceal me in His tabernacle; in the secret place of His tent, He will hide me. He will lift me up on a rock" (Psalm 27:5).

My friend also shared that it would be difficult to focus and, at times, it would feel as though I were losing my mind. Again, what a relief, because I did feel as if I were losing my mind! I remembered a promise of God given by Paul: "For God has not given us a spirit of fear, but of power and of love and of a sound mind" (2 Timothy 1:7 NKJV). I couldn't focus very well to pray at that time, so I simply repeated, "Keep my mind sound, Lord; guard it. Help me, hold me." I would wake the next morning and say, "Thank you, thank you for holding me." Then the prayer for help would continue throughout the day. I prayed those words incessantly for months.

I did numb my mind in other ways, as well. I spent a few hours of every day for several months staring at the television. I watched HGTV sell homes and Dr. Phil give advice to anorexics. I then turned to Oprah applauding entrepreneurs for making millions simply because they willed it to happen. It was mind-numbing, which is just what I wanted. I wanted to numb out my thoughts and grief. Grief is undeniably the most exhausting, arduous journey I have ever faced. One can be overcome by grief, and time can somehow get lost when grief sets in.

Another way to experience numbness is anti-anxiety medicine. Several months before Kristen died, a doctor prescribed anti-anxiety pills for me. I was in such despair that, during any conversation, I would dissolve in tears and cry at length. The doctor suggested I take the anti-anxiety pills for those times. A dear friend, who is also a nurse, noticed the increased frequency of my need. She explained that anti-anxiety pills are temporary fixes that calm a person; however, the medicine wears off quickly, which then causes an intense need for more. Anti-anxiety drugs can become addictive over time. She advised that I see a new doctor. I stopped taking the anti-anxiety pills and met with a new doctor.

The second doctor explained to me that the three years of crises had created stress which depleted my brain of serotonin, a chemical needed for a stable mood. Anti-depressants do not provide temporary fixes or create intense addictions, as the anti-anxiety medications do. Anti-depressants simply cause the serotonin level to rise and restore stability. This medication is not taken whenever one feels upset, but rather once a day to continue toward one goal—replenish what was depleted. The doctor worked with me as I tried a few different types, over a period of months, before finding one that worked. I continued taking the anti-depressant medication for a couple of years.

I wrote in my journal,

> I must continually focus on the glory of God. I must fill the void within me with who God is and what He has done and what He promises He will do in the future. I can fill the void of why God said no to me by joining the angels and saying, "Holy, holy, holy is the Lord God Almighty, who was and who is and who is to come, and worthy is the Lamb who was slain."

In September, I rejoined the Bible Study for women at our church. I forced myself to get up on Tuesdays. It helped to put one foot in front of the other, knowing I could return home later that day and rest. It was difficult to focus at times, yet I wanted to walk the steady course I had always walked. I also appreciated the encouragement of meeting with friends each week at the study.

In October, I came up with a creative idea to sharpen my brain rather than numb it. I had sewn for many years and decided to make matching pajamas for my three grandsons. I also made a nightgown for my granddaughter Megan that matched one I made for my daughter, Rebecca. It was a project that took several weeks, and it did engage the creative side of my brain. I kept it a secret from Erica and looked forward to seeing my little ones.

And then, we had our first Christmas without Kristen. The firsts are difficult; from the first holiday to the first birthday to the first anniversary of saying goodbye. We were advised to change things up when the firsts came. David took that advice seriously and wanted to get far away. He left for Australia with a friend for two weeks. We were so grateful to have Sam with us for this first Christmas without Kristen. We spent several days in San Antonio with Erica and her family— and the matching pajamas were a hit!

After that first Christmas, John and I went together to GriefShare at our church. GriefShare is a nationwide 13-week grief recovery support group. After a few weeks, John said he didn't feel a need to continue. I understood that we were reacting differently to loss, and I finished the course on my own. Grief has its own agenda in the life of each person. It comes in waves, without warning, and cannot be scheduled in or held back.

John and I both lost our daughter and we both were enveloped in shock and grief. Yet, we discovered that our grief journeys and feelings were completely different. John felt better by following the routine of his day and immersing himself in his job. John has always been reticent regarding his feelings. He would dream about Kristen and the next morning gulp and blink tears away just to be able to say only, "I had a dream last night." I, on the other hand, would have a dream and share it in detail, along with every feeling I was experiencing. Grief is a solitary journey; it helped to have my husband by my side and to talk to friends, but ultimately, I walked this solitary journey with my best friend, Jesus.

There is a promise in the Bible that many rely on when they have little strength to continue their journey. Isaiah 40:30-31 states, "Those who wait for the Lord will gain new strength. They will mount up with wings like eagles; they will run and not get tired; they will walk and not faint." The thought of being given the strength of a soaring eagle is a promise worth considering. No other bird can fly as high as an eagle. Eagles are able to use the wind pressure of a raging storm to gain altitude. They then can actually rest, conserve energy, and soar on the built-up pressure for long distances. To be given the strength to rise above the grief, to glide above the pressure toward a light-filled sky is almost an incomprehensible notion when one is inside the shadow.

But wait! The verse continues after the promise of the eagle and gives two other ways God will give new strength. "Those who wait for the Lord will gain new strength...they will run and not get tired; they will walk and not faint." During the three years of Kristen's cancer, God gave all who loved her the strength to run and not get tired. We ran from one crisis to another with His strength. We did rely on God's second promise in this verse.

It is a worthy pursuit to ask God for the third way He promises strength: "They will walk and not faint." I began to gain strength as I contemplated that phrase. I took encouragement once again from author John Claypool. He writes about this passage:

> In the kind of darkness where I have been, it is the only form of the promise that fits the situation. When there is no occasion to soar and no place to run; and all you can do is to edge along step by step, to hear of a Help that will enable you to "walk and not faint" is good news indeed. It not only corresponds

to the limits of the situation, it also speaks
to the greatest difficulty; namely, "to hang in
there"...in the dark stretches of life, the most
difficult discipline of all is not that of soaring
or even of running. It consists of "keep on
keeping on" when events have slowed you
to a walk, when it seems that in spite of
everything you are going to crumple under
the load and faint away.[21]

Chapter Fourteen

STAGES

I can count a million times
people asking me how I
praise You with all that I've gone through.
The question just amazes me.
Can circumstances possibly
change who I forever am in You.[22]

Several decades ago, a book was written which stated that the stages of grief were shock, anger, despair, depression, and acceptance. I had come to despise the word *stages*. We had progressed through several stages of cancer and now there were more stages facing me. I didn't like to think of grief in stages, as though I should close a stage door and step onto the next stage.

One of the counselors that I spoke with during that time told me that grief is fluid. I found this to be the truer statement. Shock was fluid within me for months. I would think that the shock had ended and weeks would pass. Then I would find myself in disbelief once again as random thoughts would come, such as, "I am one of those moms who had a child die of cancer! I watched my sweet child lose her hair and her physical stamina. I witnessed her liver bulging while the rest of her became skeletal. I watched my child die a slow, painful death! Then, I watched her take her last breath!"

Actually, I believe a stage of grief should be added. It should be called the "illogical, random thoughts" stage. Illogical, random thoughts would pop into my mind like unwanted ads on a computer screen. I would entertain the "if only" thoughts. "If only we could have, or if only we would have, or we should have done something different or something more" are thoughts that plague many after the death of a loved one, and I was no different than the many.

One morning an illogical random thought surfaced and led me back in time to when I began giving Kristen vegetables. Rather than purchasing baby food, I had pureed canned vegetables for her. The illogical, random thought about the vegetables surfaced in my grief and I immediately decided there were no nutrients in the can! The immediate next thought came—if only I had fed her better, she would not have gotten cancer. I swirled and twirled on the "illogical, random thoughts" stage for some time.

I would feel the fluid stage of anger each October—Breast Cancer Awareness Month. Glorified stories of courageous champions who triumphed in their battle permeate the media throughout the month every year. The accounts include how these champions have the will to live and somehow have a power within themselves to survive. Physical fitness and healthy eating are often attributed to their longevity. The endless accounts of victory ignore those who were equally courageous yet did not survive. Kristen had an indomitable spirit and she battled mightily. She was physically active and healthy throughout her life. She was young and vibrant and had the will to live!

The stories of courageous survivors bothered me because God is not typically factored into their victory. Because we are this side of heaven, we don't fully know God's plan for us. When the diagnosis comes, it is right to fight the good fight. It is good to pray and ask others to join us in prayer. We use the best technology that God has allowed man to develop, and meet with the best specialists. We follow through on every protocol that is available to us. We take the chemo and the radiation, we diet and exercise and swallow the herb drinks. It is good and right to pursue all of the above, but we still don't fully know God's plan for us.

The God factor is given to us throughout His Word: "Surely, just as I have intended so it has happened, and just as I have planned so it will stand" (Isaiah 14:24). The Bible also states in Job 14:6, "His days are determined. The number of his months is with Thee and his limits Thou has set so that he cannot pass." Throughout October, I want to shout these words of God to all mankind: "See now that I, I am He, and there is no god besides Me. It is I who put to death and give life. I have wounded and it is I who heal" (Deuteronomy 32:39).

One year in October, the local Christian radio station spent the month highlighting survivor stories. The phrase, "God **does** answer prayer" was proclaimed as each story was celebrated and God was praised for the answer "YES." I would vehemently want to correct this one-dimensional view of praising God simply because He answered yes to a request. It could lead some to believe that either God doesn't hear or God doesn't care when prayers are not given the desired answer. When we pray and do not get the answer we desire, it is **not** due to the fact that God did not answer us. Billy Graham writes,

> We cannot explain why some withered bodies are healed while others suffer and die. We cannot know why some prayers seem so wonderfully answered and others seemingly go unheard. We cannot pretend that life in Christ always means victory, miracle, and success in this life. When we tell only the stories of victory, we tell only a part of the truth. When we recount only the answered prayers, we oversimplify life in Christ.[23]

I want to shout out in praise to the God of the "No!" He is worthy to be praised regardless of His answer. God does answer prayer and sometimes He says "No" to our persistent, prevailing prayers. It is difficult to be at the receiving end, but God also gives His enduring strength to those who hear "No." And, most importantly, I want to shout out that God is to be praised because He is the all-powerful Ancient of Days, Who Was, Who Is, and Who Is to come, Almighty God, not just because He said yes to a prayer!

The stages of despair and depression were, at times, intense and always integral to my anguish for my sweet grandson, Sam. I physically ached that this young child could not grasp his loss. David said that Sam would search through the house—double-checking the bedroom—looking for his mother. I ached that he had his mother for a short eighteen months, only to have this generous, indescribable gift of love meant to nurture him taken away. During the first several months, Sam would cling to me when Fridays came. I sensed that he associated me in some way with his missing mom. The three of us had spent so many days together in the months before her passing. Our voices sounded so much alike that people often mistook us for the other on the phone. I knew that Sam could hear the intonation of his mother's voice when I spoke to him.

Incredibly, David was able to take a six-month leave of absence from work when Kristen died so that he could care for Sam. But this idyllic setting ended and Sam began daycare at a Montessori preschool. For several weeks, when he was placed into my car by the day care worker on Fridays, he would reach for me and begin to cry. He would cry until he was gagging and choking. After driving to the other side of the parking lot and taking him out of his car seat, I would hold him and gently talk to him until he calmed. He didn't understand his new routine. It was torment to me! I would cry out to God, "This is a **good plan**?"

It was torment, but, at the same time, I was grateful for every Friday. Eventually, Sam's grief dissipated. John and I continued to be another source of love to Sam. We could offer the respite to David and become a support to him, as well. Once Sam adjusted, we all looked forward to Fridays. Occasionally, David would need to be gone the whole weekend and Sam would excitedly say, "Double overnight, double overnight!"

God did bring a precious gift to us in the midst of our grief. Emma Kristen, Erica and Jonathan's fourth child, was born in the year after Kristen's death. She is a happy child who brings laughter to us with her silliness. Each of my grandchildren is a precious treasure to me and being in their presence immediately lifts my spirit. I took a positive step away from the depths of my grief when I placed a 3 x 5 card in front of their pictures with the following verse from Philippians 1:21-24: "For to me to live is Christ, and to die is gain. But if I am to live on in the flesh, this will mean fruitful labor for me...I am hard pressed from both directions...yet to remain on in the flesh is more necessary for your sake."

A friend who was experiencing her own adversity shared with me her morning routine. She asked herself each morning, "What do I know to be the truth this day?" She would then list out some Biblical truths, such as "I am a child of God" (Romans 8:17), "I am inseparable from God's love" (Romans 8:35), and "He will never leave me nor forsake me" (Hebrews 13:5). She intentionally shifted her focus to truth rather than feelings. If we lived solely on our feelings, most of us would not get out of bed!

In my journal, I wrote,

> My pain and sorrow lies dormant now for periods of time. Then it resurfaces and I am weak, confused, and engulfed in grief. I have to remember whose I am and recall truth. I stay hidden in Christ, even now. I recall that He promised to cocoon me. My truth for today is that I am hidden with Christ in God (Colossians 3:3).

Chapter Fifteen

HEAVEN

Come out of sadness
From wherever you've been
Come brokenhearted
Let rescue begin
Come find your mercy
Oh sinner come kneel
Earth has no sorrow
That Heaven can't heal.

Earth has no sorrow
That Heaven can't heal.[24]

Gradually, over a five-year period, the constant presence of agony began to dissipate ever so slowly, and I was able to think more clearly. I no longer wore the heavy blanket of dread. Sun continually broke through the shadow.

My irrational thoughts and emotions became less troubled. However, an ache in my heart still remains. The sorrow of losing my child is forever interwoven with all the other character traits that define me.

Sorrow took me to a frightening darkness that caused a deeper level of dependency on my Savior than I could ever imagine possible. Sorrow refined my hard edges and caused me to have compassion for others who suffer. Sorrow is now integrated into my emotional DNA. Sorrow redefined me. Many have gone before me and many will follow after me on a grief journey. Grief is an incredible journey of being held by Christ. It is an incredible training ground for growth, as well. Elizabeth Elliot once wrote,

> When Jesus said that those who mourn, those who are poor and persecuted and have nothing are 'blessed', He was saying this in light of another kingdom, another way of seeing this world. He came to bring life— another kind of life altogether. It is in terms of that life that we must learn to look at our suffering...I have found it possible, when I see suffering from that perspective, but it takes a steady fixing of my gaze on the cross.[25]

I still choose to recall daily that God's ways are not my ways. I make active, daily choices to steadily fix my gaze on the cross.

During the initial impact of grief, many people do not want to focus on the glorious reality of their loved one being with Christ. I was definitely one of those people. I didn't want to hear the encouraging phrases from others saying, "Rejoice, you know she is in Heaven!" For some, fresh grief is not soothed by thoughts of "where." I knew where she was—I wasn't okay with "where!" I either wanted her with me or I wanted to be in heaven with her! Ever so slowly, I began to entertain the thoughts of Kristen with Jesus. I could finally think on her without longing to be with her. I found words of Ann Voskamp very encouraging:

> How can God ever expect us to say goodbye to the eyes, ears, and hands of those we cherish more than our own? Is it because His heart awaits us at home? Because if we don't say goodbye here, when will we meet Him there? Because these are the lens words for a life from Psalm 116:15: "precious in His eyes is the homecoming of the Saints."[26]

As time passed, I was able to focus on the true reality that God is on the throne where worship is occurring right now. I was able to ponder that Kristen is joining in that worship.

Those who trust in Christ are "citizens of Heaven" who will be "transformed so that they are like Jesus' glorious body" (Philippians 3:20-21). They will be "raised in power with imperishable bodies" (1 Corinthians 15:42-43). They will have found the "better country, that is a heavenly one... prepared by God" (Hebrews 11:16). In Heaven, they will have a mind that "knows fully, just as God now knows us fully" (1 Corinthians13:12).

Tada and Estes write,

> Suffering turns our hearts toward the future, like a mother turning the face of her child, insisting, "look this way!" Once heaven has our attention, a fervid anticipation for God's ultimate reality—appearing with Him in glory —begins to glow, making everything earthly pale in comparison. Earth's pain keeps crushing our hopes, reminding us this world can never satisfy; only heaven can.[27]

John Claypool read through the book of Job to study how one person coped with the experience that is common to all of us. Again, he put into words my own thoughts as I approached year five: "In a real sense our grief experience is a 'Gethsemane' where we are brought face to face with the necessity of saying: 'Here is what I want. Nevertheless, not my will but Thine be done.'"[28]

We can study how one person copes in the Bible. We can observe others who are experiencing grief. These are very helpful. Yet, a grief journey has its own agenda and its own time line. It is a solitary walk through the valley of the shadow of death that one person takes—even within a family. A favorite quote of mine was written decades ago in an allegory by Hannah Hurnard. I wrote it out and laminated it to keep it in mind.

> Others have gone this way before me and they could even sing about it afterward. Will he who is so strong and gentle be less faithful and gracious to me, weak and cowardly though I am, when it is obvious that the thing he delights in most of all is to deliver his followers from all their fears and to take them to the High Places?[29]

Many others have taken the free fall plunge when a loved one dies and have found themselves inside the shadow of the valley of death. Psalm 23 gives a promise that God will be with those who mourn. He will give mourners the strength to walk through—rather than stay inside—the shadow. *Through* is the key word, even though I could not fathom this five years earlier when my journey began. My yearning for any who find themselves inside the shadow is that they also walk with Jesus Christ. He is faithful to give His strength to the one who grieves. He is a strong tower that can be leaned on when believers experience intense emotions of fear, dread, or anger and bitterness during their grief. Psalm 34:18 is a sure promise to recall: "The Lord is near to the brokenhearted and saves those who are crushed in spirit." This is a promise to stand on while inside the shadow. He is faithful to give His strength to the one who grieves, even when one holds onto a blanket of dread.

Grief counselors explain that, at some point, those in grief will begin to recognize times during the year that bring sad memories. From early May through June, the fragrant flowers and hint of the heat of summer bring memories of Kristen's final days. I have bittersweet emotions as the crepe myrtles in my backyard begin to bud. Kristen's birthday is December 28, so the Christmas holiday brings with it an ache that there is someone missing. I do remember and rejoice and thank God for those who are present. Nevertheless, I am always aware of the memories of rejoicing over my second born so many years ago.

King Solomon once said, "God has set eternity in the hearts of men, yet men cannot fathom what God has done from beginning to end" (Ecclesiastes 3:11). We were made to live forever, so this break from Kristen's presence—from her voice and her laughter and her touch—is unnatural to the eternal in any who knew her. God hardwired us to long for something beyond this life—eternity. Even though we all experience a break from Kristen's presence, she did not experience any break or any loss of love. In the twinkling of an eye, she stepped away from this earth, and she continues to walk in newness of life. Her voice, her laughter, and her touch continue on in the presence of Jesus Christ.

I continue to thank God today that, in His infinite eternal plan, Christ would be the firstborn from the dead and, because of His death and resurrection, all who believe in Him will follow, as Kristen did on June 7, 2005. Jesus promises that one day He will return to take all those who love Him. We will go to be with Him. A great day of celebration, referred to as a wedding day with a feast, will occur. Jesus will set all things right, and there will be no more physical breaks from love. I look forward to that wedding day and the day the prophecy of Revelation 21 will be fulfilled:

> Then I saw a new heaven and a new earth... and I heard a loud voice from the throne saying, "Now the dwelling of God is with men, and he will live with them. They will be his people, and God himself will be with them and be their God. He will wipe every tear from their eyes. There will be no more death or mourning or crying or pain, for the old order of things has passed away." He who was seated on the throne said, "I am making everything new!" Then He said, "Write this down, for these words are trustworthy and true."

These trustworthy words were said to John by Jesus Christ. Regarding this promise from Christ, Randy Alcorn writes, "We can count on them and live in light of them. We were all made for a person and a place. Jesus is the person and heaven is the place."[30]

I can hear it in the distance
and it's not too far away
it's the music and the laughter
of a wedding and a feast.

I can almost feel the hand of God
reaching for my face
to wipe the tears away, and say,
"It's time to make everything new."

Out of these ashes...beauty will rise
and we will dance among the ruins
we will see Him with our own eyes.
Out of this darkness...new life will shine
and we'll know the joy is coming in the morning.
In the morning...beauty will rise.[31]

EPILOGUE

E veryone asks. Everyone wants to know how David and Sam are doing. Did David remarry?

Several years ago, a young couple went skiing in Vermont. The young man, Edd, collided with a tree. Within the twinkling of an eye, this incredibly healthy, vibrant, and amazing man's heart stopped beating. Within the twinkling of an eye, the dynamics and future of an entire family were changed forever. His wife, Claudine, became a widow. His two young sons would mourn and miss their dad. His newborn baby girl would not remember the daddy who held her and loved her dearly. His parents and his sisters would grieve the loss of their only son and brother. Their grief journey had begun.

At some point during her grief journey, Claudine shared with a friend that she would prefer to date a widower with children—one who would know the loss of a cherished life partner. One who would empathize with raising children alone. Claudine's friend told a friend who told another friend who emailed another friend until Claudine and David met.

When Claudine and David married, their children were 2, 4, 6, and 8, with Sam being the oldest brother. Before the ceremony, pealing bells rang out fluidly and joyfully from the steeple sounding almost like rippling waters of happiness. I later noted in the program that the bells were rung to honor Kristen and Edd. During the wedding, the pastor said, "We thank God today; He took two tragedies and created a family."

I had begun to pray for this possibility a couple of years after Kristen died. I mainly prayed that God would prepare me and bring me to a place of acceptance so that I could rejoice with those who rejoice. I also prayed that God would bring a mom to Sam who would love him so much that a mother/son bond would form. I was concerned David would marry someone who had no children and would not understand the ways of a very active boy. God answered my prayers with a mom of boys. David and Claudine added another boy to their new family, so Sam now has three brothers and one sister. I am so glad that Claudine is a mom who searches to know the blueprint of her children. Sam loves his new mom and I am grateful to God for Claudine.

HOLDING HANDS

The first time I held her hand she was minutes old. I was in awe that, only moments before, she had been a part of me and now she was her own little self. I held her tiny baby hand in mine. It struck me that her long delicate fingers reminded me of my grandmother's. She was my precious child.

When she was seven, Kristen went through a phase of being frightened at night. She would beg me to stay with her and hold her hand till she fell asleep. I would kneel by her bed and hold her sweet child hand in mine. Every few minutes her eyes would flutter open to reassure herself that I was still there, and, of course, I was. She was my precious child and I loved her dearly.

When she was twenty-eight, cancer won its battle. We were told that Kristen would be leaving us soon. While she was in a deep sleep, I knelt by her bed and took her grown-woman hand in mine. After some time, her eyes opened and the final conversation between us took place. She asked, "Why are you here and why are you holding my hand?" I replied, "I'm here because I love you and I love holding your hand." I held her hand throughout that day and the next until she stepped out of this life. She, who was once a part of me, now lives with Christ in eternity. She was my precious child, I loved her dearly, and I always will.

NOTES

Chapter One

1. Jonas Myrin and Matt Redman, "10,000 Reasons," *Sing Like Never Before*, CD (Sparrow Records, 2012), Track 1.

Chapter Two

2. Mark Hull and Bernie Herms, "Praise You in the Storm," *Lifesong*, CD (Beach Street and Reunion Records, 2005), Track 2.

Chapter Three

3. Carolina Sandell-Berg, "Day by Day," 1865. Andrew L Skoog., translator, English text, 1921. *The Hymnal for Worship & Celebration* (Word Music, 1986), 56.
4. Toby McKeehan, Aaron Rice, Jamie Moore, and Cary Barlowe, "Made to Love You," *Portable Sounds*, CD (Forefront Records, 2006), Track 2.

Chapter Four

5. Philip Yancey, *Where is God When it Hurts?* (Grand Rapids: Zondervan Publishers, 1990), 84.
6. Irish text, 6th Century, "Be Thou My Vision." Mary Byrne, translator, English text, 1912. *The Hymnal for Worship & Celebration*. (Word Music, 1986), 382.

Chapter Five

7. Benton Kevin Stokes and Tony Wood, "Sometimes He Calms the Storm," *Wild Imagination*, CD (Word Records, 1995), Track 4.

8. Ibid.

Chapter Six

9. Yancey, *Where Is God When It Hurts?* 47.

Chapter Eight

10. Daniel Carson, Christy Nockels, Nathan Nockels, Matt Redman, Chris Tomlin, "Healing is in Your Hands," *Passion Awakening*, CD (Sixstepsrecords, 2010), Track 5.

Chapter Nine

11. John Waller III, "While I'm Waiting," *While I'm Waiting*, CD (Provident Music, 2009), Track 3.

Chapter Ten

12. Matt Redman and Beth Redman, "You Never Let Go," *Beautiful News*, CD (Sixstepsrecords, 2006), Track 2.

13. Ibid.

Chapter Eleven

14. Stephen Curtis Chapman, "Heaven is the Face," *Beauty Will Rise*, CD (Sparrow Records, 2009), Track 1.

15. John R. Claypool, *Tracks of a Fellow Struggler* (New Orleans: Morehouse Publishing, 1974), 51, 53.

16. Eliza E. Hewitt, "When We All Get To Heaven," 1898. *The Hymnal for Worship & Celebration* (Word Music, 1986), 542.

Chapter Twelve

17. Mercy Me, "The Hurt and the Healer," *The Hurt and the Healer*, CD (INO Records, 2012), Track 3.
18. Joni Eareckson Tada and Steven Estes, *When God Weeps* (Grand Rapids: Zondervan Publishers, 1997), 202.
19. Ibid., 125.

Chapter Thirteen

20. Chapman, "With Hope," *Speechless*, CD (Sparrow Records, 1999), Track 9.
21. Claypool, *Tracks of a Fellow Struggler*, 37-38.

Chapter Fourteen

22. Mercy Me, "Bring the Rain," *Coming Up to Breathe*, CD (INO Records, 2006), Track 8.
23. Billy Graham, *Approaching Hoofbeats* (Waco: Word Books Publishers, 1983), 94.

Chapter Fifteen

24. David Crowder, Matt Maher and Ben Glover, "Come as You Are," *Neon Steeple*, CD (Sparrow Records and Sixsteprecords, 2014), Track 6.
25. Elizabeth Elliot, *A Path Through Suffering* (Ann Arbor: Servant Publications, 1990), 25.
26. Ann Voskamp, *One Thousand Gifts* (Grand Rapids: Zondervan Publishers, 2010), 93.
27. Eareckson and Estes, *When God Weeps,* 202.
28. Claypool, *Tracks of a Fellow Struggler,* 87.
29. Hannah Hurnard, *Hind's Feet on High Places* (Wheaton: Barbour and Company, 1977), 68.

30. Randy Alcorn, *Heaven* (Wheaton: Tyndale House Publishers, 2004), 457.

31. Chapman, "Beauty Will Rise," *Beauty Will Rise*, CD (Sparrow Records, 2009), Track 2.

CPSIA information can be obtained
at www.ICGtesting.com
Printed in the USA
LVOW05s0853200316

479957LV00039B/179/P